HOW TO PLAY
LINKS
GOLF

A special thanks to Rick Vershure, head golf professional of Quaker Ridge Golf Club, Scarsdale, New York, for his help in reading the copy and making sure that teaching concepts are clearly presented.

Thanks also to Nick Seitz and Bruce Smith for proofreading and refining the manuscript.

FIRST EDITION

ISBN 1-888531-09-6

Published by:
The American Golfer
200 Railroad Avenue
Greenwich, Connecticut 06830
203-862-9720 (Tel)
203-862-9724 (Fax)
imd@aol.com (E-mail)

Instructional Photographs by:
Andrew Redington, AllSport
All other photos by AllSport,
unless otherwise noted

Designed by:
Lisa Richards
GraphixWorks
51 Hemlock Trail
Trumbull, Connecticut 06611
203-377-3647 (Tel)

Film and Separations by:
Gateway Graphics
140 Water Street
Norwalk, Connecticut 06854
203-853-4929 (Tel)

For John Laupheimer
and John Morris,
two great friends of golf.

HOW TO PLAY
LINKS GOLF

by **Martin Davis**

INSTRUCTION
by **Colin Montgomerie**

and the Turnberry Professional Staff

in conjunction with the British PGA

IN PRAISE
& CELEBRATION
OF LINKS
by **Donald Steel**

The American Golfer, Inc. • 200 Railroad Avenue • Greenwich, Connecticut 06830

tel 203-862-9720 • fax 203-862-9724 • e-mail imd@aol.com

TABLE OF CONTENTS

IN PRAISE &
CELEBRATION OF
LINKS

by Donald Steel

Researching the origins of golf is as pointless as trying to discover who invented bread. Furthermore, there is a danger that, in attempting such an investigation, the delights of both could be overlooked. There is another stumbling block. If research were to be carried out by an historian, his erudite findings may pass over the heads of most of his readers; if by a layman, he may be too ignorant of history to be taken seriously.

Nobody will ever know where, when and by whom the first golf shot was played. The truth is it really doesn't matter. However, what is totally beyond dispute is that the first recognized courses occupied the remarkable stretches of sand and sand hills punctuating the coastline of the British Isles, land that came to be known in the golfing vocabulary as links.

Remarkable stretches of land and sand hills punctuating the coastline of the British Isles came to be known as links...

Quite why nature bestowed this rare blessing is another matter that needn't concern us either. Scientific explanations would require volumes to do justice to the subject. Suffice to say, that land built up over centuries as the seas retreated. Hills

Ireland's contribution followed, its links being the equal of anything anywhere. As a result, it is from these simple beginnings that many of the game's traditions gained a foothold. But one point of clarification is due. Why were the early courses

The grasses were, by nature, fine and wiry, kept sparse by golf's first green keepers, the sheep.

formed subsequently to act as stout sea defenses. Wild grasses and flowers slowly took root as seeds, borne by birds and winds off the land, germinated.

The grasses were, by nature, fine and wiry, kept sparse by golf's first green keepers, the sheep. Grazing was, in fact, the land's only practical use. But nature's wizardry didn't stop there. In places, crumpled valleys emerged between the sand dunes to provide ribbons of fairway, and the hollows that developed, again the handiwork of the sheep, provided ready-made bunkers. By this somewhat haphazard process, golf's heritage was forged and bequeathed to Britain although

termed "links"? Many theories have been expounded. Whether mine is right or wrong, I cannot swear, but it is at least plausible and convenient. It refers quite literally to the terrain linking the sea with more fertile plains – often a strip no more than 200 yards wide. Any definition of links will say correctly that it has to be a seaside course but, by no means, are all links characterized by sand dunes.

When our forefathers, who started playing the game across country, were looking for more confined spaces in which to pursue their new sport, links fitted the bill admirably. Gradually, as the game spread farther, links were looked upon as role models, a situation that still pertains among right thinking golfers. Down the ages, golf course architects have worshiped at their shrines. First and foremost to claim attention was the Old Course at St Andrews but other early nurseries were Prestwick, Musselburgh, North Berwick, Hoylake, Westward Ho!, Aberdeen and Dornoch. Cruden Bay or Nairn or Sandwich were also founts of influence.

Ben Hogan, who came, saw and conquered Carnoustie in 1953.

Golf therefore joined whisky as Scotland's most famous exports although golfers may be divided over which has given more lasting benefit. Some depend on both. Another unanswered question is why golf courses popped up all around our shores and yet took a couple of centuries to venture into the heart lands. In the early days, when travel was long and laborious, golf could only be enjoyed at the seaside.

By the very nature of their location, links are imbued with a feeling of remoteness and isolation, invariably in an exposed setting. Theirs can be a bleak beauty, a barren landscape with scarcely a tree in sight, a striking contrast to the more sheltered splendor of, say, an Augusta National. However, some links are unbelievably scenic, a case of the frame being more beautiful than the picture itself. Turnberry,

Royal County Down, Royal Dornoch, Waterville— everybody can produce their own mouth watering list.

It is a common belief that traditional links are the only true form of expression and that anything else scarcely deserves mention in the same breath. The Royal and Ancient Golf Club set the trend by staging every Open championship on a links,

Theirs can be a bleak beauty, a barren landscape with scarcely a tree in sight.

and there is absolutely no sign of any chink in their loyalty. They do so on account of the infinite variety that links present, all the great players returning the compliment by feeling a need, indeed a duty, to prove they have the skills and the mental resilience to overcome what, to many, are alien conditions. The most notable example was Ben Hogan in 1953 who came, saw and conquered Carnoustie in, sadly, his lone appearance in the championship. Everyone knew he was the master but, without his epic victory, he knew his mastery would never be acknowledged in the record books as complete.

Bobby Jones won the Amateur championship in 1930 and the Open championship in 1926, 1927 and 1930.

The Royal and Ancient Golf Club.

Golf's face has changed constantly through the ages but the game today is in danger of becoming more science than art or, to be more precise, the conditions under which it is played are becoming too stereotyped. Caddies, armed with a plethora of charts, measure everything to the inch. Obsession with manicured courses, emerald green wall to wall, places undue emphasis on irrigation and chemicals. Too much advantage is to be gained by the ability to carry the ball vast distances in order to obey the whim of contemporary design, and there is a growing reluctance among golfers to accept that bad bounces are as essential an ingredient as the good.

Happily absolved from such censure are links. Links are the embodiment of what a good course should look like although invariably there are few identifying features. Many a pilgrim has peered out from the 1st tee on the Old Course at St Andrews wondering what all the fuss is about.

Bobby Jones took time to accept its strategic charm and Arnold Palmer expressed uncertainty at first glance but both were quick to learn, laud and appreciate the subtle, thinking approach that it demands.

The Old Course is unique in so many ways, but the precious message conveyed by links golf is a collective one that, like stirring music, can bear hearing again and again. So what are the special virtues of its mystique?

…golf is a game of constant decision-making, the relevance of having several options highlighting the fact that, spoilt for choice, it is easier to take the wrong one…

First, that colour is no yardstick of quality. Secondly, that the ball should actually run when it lands and that the art of control and positional play is a surer sign of skill than raw power. Improvisation, ingenuity and invention are also key requisites of a golfer's make-up, qualities that receive greater expression on a links than elsewhere. Links offer options and choices about how a particular hole or a particular stroke should be tackled. Golf is a game of constant decision-making, the relevance of having several options highlighting the fact that, spoilt for choice, it is easier to take the wrong one. This is the situation that

breeds self-doubt, the greatest destructive force in the game.

It is specially the case around the green where the smart choice is frequently a shot with the putter. What a contrast to the situation on other courses set up for big events when the penalty for the merest blemish is no shot at all.

With a virtual absence of trees, vegetation on links consists almost entirely of deep-rooted bushes and wispy grasses blown in the wind, epitomizing their vast open canvases. The sense of escape evoked by this feeling underlines the fact that only a tiny handful of golfers play golf to meet its ultimate competitive challenge. The majority do so for healthy exercise, the joy of being alive and the sheer enjoyment of the beauty in which they find themselves.

Irrigation and modern playing equipment have undoubtedly brought about some changes in the way links are prepared and tackled. For centuries, their condition was literally in the lap of the Gods but, whatever the season, golfers' instincts are more concerned with keeping the ball low and, when expedient, favor the bump and run to a high, lofted approach. Peter Thomson, five times Open champion, and a celebrated lover and exponent of links, struck the perfect note in a Foreword he wrote for *Classic Links of Great Britain and Ireland.*

He spoke of "the thrill of squeezing the ball against the firm turf, trying to

keep it low into a buffeting wind, something that lingers in the mind forever. It reminds me, too, that a good deal of golf is played on the ground, or at least it should be. Classic golf provides this. There is a lot of chipping and long putting to do. Approaches can be made with straight-faced irons, running the ball up little banks and through shallow hollows. It is an important part of the game, alas little understood and appreciated and now, in modern design, virtually ignored."

Nor is Thomson's a lone voice. Tiger Woods, for all his prodigious hitting, is a staunch ally, a fact that may catch some people by surprise. At the Open at Royal Birkdale in 1998, he made it clear that his preference was not for the stadium-type courses in America "where you just keep hitting a lob wedge" but for links. On a links, a player has the option of hitting any club in the bag. You have to be creative. You have to see the shots, feel them in your hands."

Therein is the crux, the essential difference between links and other types of course. Links demand that players visualize a shot and work out a way of implementing it and two shots are the rarely the same. On other courses, with water everywhere and tightly guarded greens, the procedure is to hit the ball heavens high and allow it to drop vertically. The fallacy of that is that good scores can only be achieved by the best players playing at their best, a tiny proportion of the world's golfers. For the rank and file, there is the inevitable sense of mission impossible.

Links demand some carries from the tee, sometimes blind shots over sand hills although blind shots are only really blind the first time they are played. For the most part, there is a good chance of finishing with the same ball that you hit off the first tee. All sorts of categories are considered nowadays in the rating of courses, an exercise which, if you will pardon the pun, is overrated.

Tiger at the Open at Royal Birkdale in 1998.

Fun and enjoyment are too often overlooked, yet nothing is more important for the increasing army of retired and senior golfers.

What makes Britain's precious legacy of links all the stranger is that it is a bequest not shared with other countries although there is still the hope of some undiscovered paradise somewhere.

There are several fine links courses along the coast of Holland.

Holland's coast has two or three fine examples and the New South Wales GC near Sydney, Australia sets the purists' pulses racing while a new haven south-east of Melbourne on the Mornington Peninsula is rapidly making a name for itself.

adjust. A hole that is a 9-iron in the morning can be a 3-wood after lunch. With usually small margins for error, straightness and accuracy find their reward.

At the same time, links, to re-emphasize the point, provide options, and nowhere more so than at St. Andrews. There are invariably two or three ways of playing holes to suit the conditions, the circumstances of the round and the state of mind of the player. Links extol the virtues of positional play coupled with the subtle art of proper angling, shaping and contouring of greens. A.W. Tillinghast, the

However, the closest equivalent to links in America is maybe a thousand miles from the sea. Nobody can attempt to build a links without the authentic raw material. Nevertheless, that does not excuse design and construction of new courses in some countries that disfigures a noble art. What Peter Dobereiner called "temples of bad taste," and costing millions and millions of dollars, are a betrayal of the fundamental lessons that links golf teaches.

Links and the wind are so inseparable that, without true striking and control, matters can soon get out of hand. Study of flight and the ability to maneuver the ball are keys to survival. Judgement, rather than dependence on a recital of yardage, is another vital ingredient together with the need to

first great, prolific American-born golf course architect, had a graphic description on the subject of greens. He maintained, "A putting green has features like a human, or, at least, it should have to be worthy of the name. Of course, there are many which are no more impressive than the vacant, cow-like expression of some people, but then again there are some with rugged

A.W. Tillinghast, the first great, prolific American born golf course architect, had a graphic description on the subject of greens.

profiles which loom head and shoulders above the common herd, and the moment we clap eyes on one of these, impulsively we murmur, 'Ah! There's a green for you!'"

shown to better effect than by the Old Course at St. Andrews. When the flags are in the kindest spots, the Old Course can be positively benign but, when the situation demands, they can be tucked into elusive corners. It is true that, with the modern preference for flying the ball high, their defense is not as water-tight as it used to be but is a reminder of the desirability everywhere that greens must be firm and fast.

A special aspect of classic golf is the bunkering or rather the style of bunkering. As the sheep found shelter in sandy craters, often self-carved, seaside bunkers tend be small,

The revetted, or sod-wall bunkers, are characterized by a steep face held firm by layers of turf...

That is another way of saying that courses need character in order to be memorable. Character, hard to define in a course but instantly recognizable, needs a whiff of eccentricity to enhance its flavor. It can take many forms and links are characterized by fairways with humps and hollows, dells and crests that rarely allow a level lie or stance. Significant rises and falls between holes are less common though by no means unknown. Royal Porthcawl, Ballybunion and parts of Royal Dornoch feature elevated sections where the views are enhanced even if the wind can be keener. Modern golfers like everything on a plate, preferably a silver salver, but, if you want to prove your superiority and powers of invention, the rumpled fairways of links are the ideal platform.

Pin placement, a subject many believe to be a relatively recent innovation, has, in fact, never been

deep and the devil of a test of recovery play. The

revetted, or sod-wall bunkers (as Americans describe them), are characterized by a steep face held firm by layers of turf, a design so patented to stop the sand from flying. Unlike the big, shallow traps elsewhere that are unworthy of the name, there is no guarantee of moving a recovery more than a few yards. It is undoubtedly wisest to avoid them, one of the most infamous examples being the Road bunker on the left front corner of the Old Course's 17th green.

Anyone who has fallen foul of it can well understand the sentiment of the old Scotsman who said, "Being in a links bunker is a little like being in an upright, hard church pew. You're not there to have a good time, you're there to atone for your sins."

Ballybunion has elevated sections where the views are enhanced even if the wind can be keener.

The links of Royal Dornoch. If you want to prove your superiority and powers of invention, the rumpled fairways of links are the ideal platform.

Although the earliest versions of links courses owed more to the hand of nature than to man, the modern adaptation of nearly all links courses bears the handiwork of a celebrated architect.

However, the message that rings loudest and clearest from their make-up is that golf course architecture has no rules. Architects use the land in the way they believe is most appropriate. There are guidelines to which most adhere but the Old Course, the blueprint, is joyfully unconventional and nobody dare say it is wrong.

How many other famous courses in the world, for instance, have only two par 3s and two par 5s? How many courses have a busy public road crossing the 1st and 18th holes? How many would tolerate a crucial tee shot passing within a few yards of a large hotel although the course predates the hotel by a few hundred years? It has double fairways and double greens, and, when many say it cannot be done, it has two holes, the 7th and 11th, that cross over. If, by crossing over, both holes in question are improved considerably, that is justification enough.

The Old Course sets the trend that, happily, courses come in shapes and sizes of all sorts. Too many courses today are built to a formula, statistical and physical, making some seem uncannily similar, but links have distinctive peculiarities far more important than worrying about having a par of 72 with two par 3s and two par 5s in each half. Another characteristic of most early links was the custom, before the days of motorized transport, of building the clubhouse closest to the town and the course with little, if any, variation in the direction in which the holes played. It was more by necessity than choice but there are notable exceptions in Muirfield, Prestwick, Royal Birkdale,

Rye, Royal St. George's, Portmarnock and Carnoustie.

It is an interesting social study how so many towns, villages and hamlets in Scotland and Ireland possess their own course, as familiar a sight as the local church or public house and maybe now more frequented. Who would have heard of Turnberry, Cruden Bay, Lahinch, Machrihanish or Ballybunion had it not been for golf? Planners in Scotland certainly recognize golf as the best way of protecting the land, the environment and the coastlines. They are comfortable with it and, if they are happy with it, why not plan-

ners everywhere? However, the basic attraction of links is the closeness of the sea.

Many spectacular holes lap the sea's edge and, on many links, the sea can be very much in play. This is an era when the building of lakes is ridiculously overdone. Links and lakes are no more homogenous than oil and water. Instead, water features on links are burns or streams or, more mundanely, ditches. The Swilcan, the Barry and the Pow Burns are illustrious names, the Pow perhaps being less well

...spectacular holes lap the sea's edge, and on many links, the sea can be very much in play...

known these days because Prestwick, the birthplace of championship golf, does not receive the same prominence on television as St. Andrews and Carnoustie.

However, Prestwick's fourth hole was arguably the first dogleg, the twist in the burn posing the conundrum for golfers of how much of the corner to cut off. For years, it was one of the most feared holes in golf. In modern golf course architecture, doglegs are a favorite feature that first established the principle of risk and reward, but this is a further example of links setting the precedent. The dramatic element in a dogleg hole lends the variety that is another integral part of a fine course, a significant contributor to overall character.

Fashions come and go but links have never gone

out of vogue, a timely reassurance that, whatever gimmickry some modern developers drum up, the bedrock is untarnished. Attempts have been made to make imitations of links, the most authentic being by Charles Blair Macdonald in the shape of The National Golf Links of America on Long Island.

An ardent lover of St. Andrews where he attended the university, he was a towering figure in the history of American golf. In his obituary in the *Times* of London in 1939, Bernard Darwin referred to his book of memories, *Scotland's Gift – Golf* as a mark of his "almost fierce loyalty to the country, which he regarded as the home of the game and from which he would brook no severance."

Darwin went on to relate how Macdonald, for 18 years a member of the Rules of Golf Committee, "hated—and there was no better hater—people who asked questions about the rules, declaring that in his youth golfers had been ruled only by the spirit of the game." He didn't offer it as Macdonald's epitaph, but Darwin added, "One of his ideals was the possession by America of a golf course built on the lines of the old classic links, and embodying all that was best in them." What is more, a statue was erected of him on the scene of his triumph. There was a reference of Darwin's that struck the perfect summary of the spirit of links.

"He hated the too eloquent advocates of 'fairness,' holding that golfers must take the bitter with the sweet, and that perfect justice would make a dull and dreary game."

That may sound nowadays an antiquated remark from a bygone age by an old reactionary. Not so. The attraction, challenge and enjoyment of links are every bit as much modern as ancient, more real than devised, fresh not faded. Their glory is timeless.

Donald Steel has been called the leading golf course architect in Europe, where he has been involved with design projects on 50 of the top 100 courses, including St. Andrews. In addition, Steel has been one of the premier golf journalists in the United Kingdom, having written for The Sunday Telegraph for 29 years. He recently completed the Kintyre Course at Turnberry, including several spectacular holes on the Firth of Clyde.

Portmarnock.

Instruction:
HOW TO PLAY
LINKS GOLF

To my way of thinking, the purest form of golf is found on the seaside links of Scotland. It's where I was born, and it's where I learned the game.

And, according to the game's historians, it's where the game began. As golfers, it's our homeland. It's our very roots. And to be able to play successfully on a links is something very, very special.

This is not to say that golf on an inland course is inferior. It's not. It's just different. But it's not like playing golf on a links.

The terrain on a links is unique. On a links course you are much more apt to get a sidehill lie or a downhill lie a after hitting a "perfect" drive, right down the middle of the fairway.

The conditions are different, too. On a links you are much more likely to encounter a great deal of wind and, of course, rain. Much more so than on an inland course.

And don't forget about the heather or gorse, the thick Scottish rough, or playing out of a steep-walled riveted bunker.

Playing on a links truly requires different skills and different shots. In the next pages, I hope to share with you some of the very specific techniques and methods that will help you succeed in playing what, to me, is the very essence of golf.

It's golf that stirs the soul. There's nothing like it.

— *Colin Montgomerie*

The 26-Shot WARM-UP DRILL

This is a marvelous way to tune-up before playing!

Loosen your upper body by doing a few stretches and by taking several practice swings. A good exercise to stretch out your lower back muscles: put a club in the crook of one elbow, put it behind your back and place the other end of the club in the crook of your other elbow. Rotate your body, imitating your golf swing.

Start with your sand iron and hit two shots, then **hit two shots** with your pitching wedge, 9-iron, etc…and **every club up to your driver**. If you have time and would like some additional work, **reverse the process** by hitting two shots with every club, starting with the driver and going back down to the sand wedge.

By the time you've finished warming-up in this way, you'll have hit every club in your bag and should feel confident going out to the course.

The 100 PUTTS Drill

This drill isn't really about holing the first 70 putts, not even the first 80, it's all about the last 15 to 20 balls. At this point, I back away from each putt, take the time to line it up carefully and really concentrate on making a solid, smooth stroke. What I'm doing, in effect, is preparing myself for the pressure of facing a putt of this length in a tournament.

This is a simple but highly effective drill for improving your putting and concentration.

Place a ball two feet from the cup and attempt to hole it. If you're successful, place a second ball in exactly the same place and again attempt to hole it. **The aim of this drill is to hole 100 consecutive putts without missing.** (You might begin this exercise with the goal of 50 straight putts. If you're comfortable with it, increase the total in subsequent practice sessions.)

If you miss one, you have to start again from zero. Although a two foot putt is relatively easy to hole, you really have to keep concentrating hard in order to hole 100 consecutive two foot putts. The pressure starts to mount as you approach the 90's because you know if you miss one, you have to start all over again.

If you regularly practice this drill, you will develop a more consistent putting stroke, your concentration levels will improve considerably and you won't miss many short putts.

Typically
Scottish Shots

On the 72nd hole of the 1988
British Open at Royal Lytham,
Seve Ballesteros hit a masterful chip
shot to secure his second Open victory.

Basic
SHORT GAME SHOTS

Given the various conditions around a links—wind, rain, thick rough, gorse, undulating fairways, firm running turf, mogul-strewn greens—the art of shot making, especially approaching and around the green, is paramount.

In the short game, it is important to play all shots with a smoothly accelerating swing. One way to reduce distance is to grip down on the club thereby reducing the length of the club. Continue using the same length swing, but the length of the shot will be slightly less for each inch the hands are moved down the club. It will be necessary to use a narrower stance each time the hands are moved downwards.

A Bump and Run— from just off the green.

Note the dominant right hand wrist hinge.

Narrow, open stance.

A Pitch Shot—
from 60 yards out.

Note the dominant right hand wrist hinge.

Slightly wider stance.

Whether it's a pitch from the fairway or a simple bump-and-run (many refer to it as a chip) from the fringe or from further down the fairway, all share the same basic principles at setup and in execution.

Jim McLean, the well-respected American teaching professional,

believes the pitch is just a bigger version of the chip, only with more wrist hinge, more swing and more footwork. With both shots, he feels that the right wrist must freely hinge on the backswing, then drops briskly as it unhinges into the ball at impact, squaring up the clubface and thus utilizing the actual loft of the

club. Everything should work freely and naturally in the swing—arms, legs and body, nothing is forced or manipulated.

Bobby Jones, pictured here in 1929, demonstrating a short pitch—narrowed stance, good wrist hinge, gripping down on the club and good footwork—just the same as taught today.

BUMP & RUN

The bump and run shot is the most commonly played chip on links courses. Generally, the shot is played from only a short distance from the edge of the green.

The principle of this shot is to take the ball from where it lies, fly it to the nearest available flat piece of green, and let it roll out to the hole from there. It is used to eliminate the unpredictable roll the ball would get through fairway or fringe length grass, making it easier to judge the pace, and, therefore, distance.

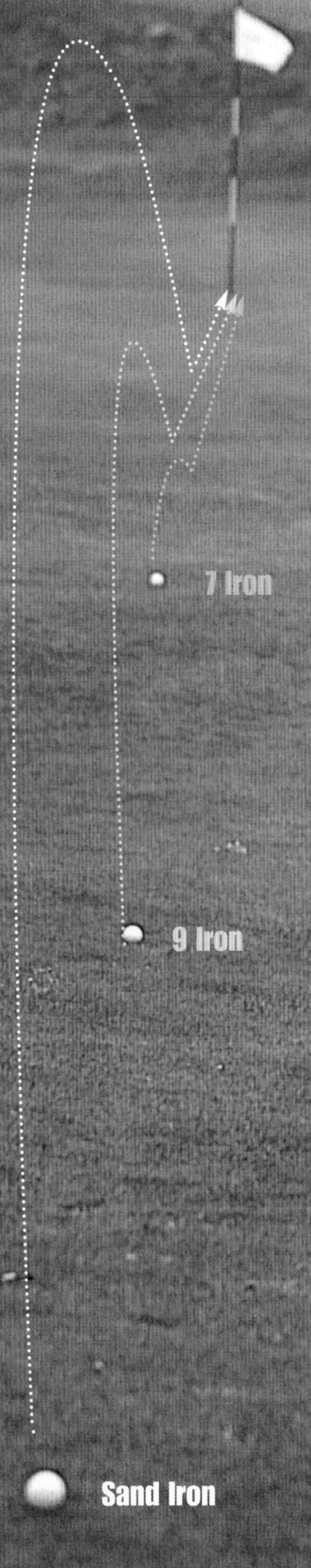

7 Iron

9 Iron

Sand Iron

When chipping around a links green, there are a number of ways that you can achieve the overall aim of getting the ball close to the pin. A lot depends on the wind. You have the option of playing a number of shots, ranging from the bump and run to the lob shot, in order to achieve the same result.

It is up to individual preference and feel as to which club you use to play the bump & run. People use either the 7, 8, or 9, pitching wedge or sand iron. You should practice with them all to get feel around the greens.

You must picture the shot—always look from the side—because distance is more important than direction.

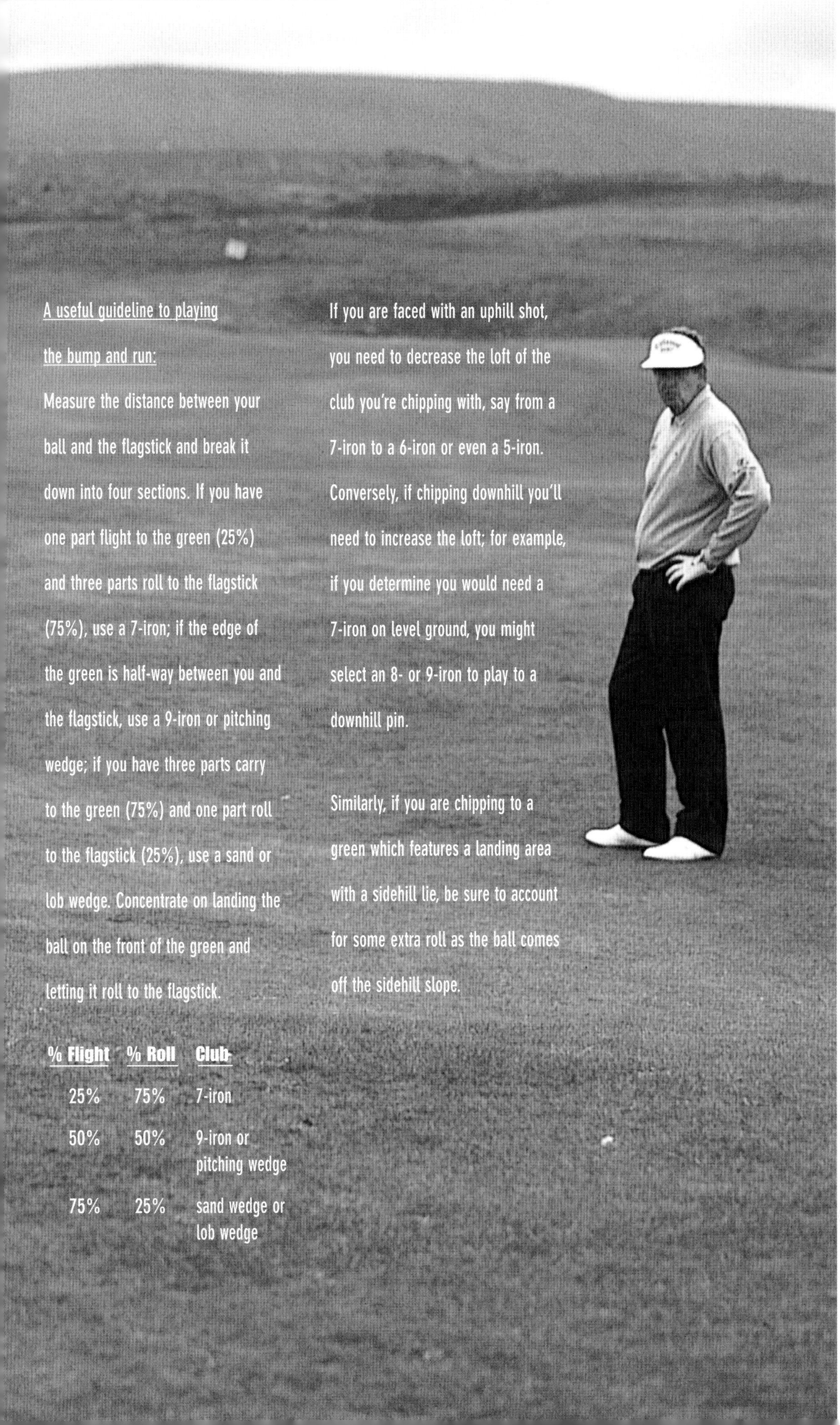

While the bump and run is usually played around the green, it can be played from much further out. Bobby Jones liked to call it the "St. Andrews" shot.

Picture a situation where you are about 50 or 60 yards out with an "open" front (no bunkers) and playing into a stiff wind. Select a four, five or six iron, play it back in a narrowed stance, hands set forward and your weight mostly on your left side. Take a waist high back swing (or less), mostly with your hands and arms, hitting down on the ball to an abbreviated, rounded low-hands finish. If the terrain is fairly flat, don't let the toe of the club pass the heel; if you have to reach an elevated green, allow the toe to pass the heel so as to impart some hook spin and hence put some additional "run" on the ball.

Practice this shot on the range varying the height of the shot, the distance to the green and the distance it scoots along the fairway. It's a great shot to have in your arsenal!

A useful guideline to playing the bump and run:

Measure the distance between your ball and the flagstick and break it down into four sections. If you have one part flight to the green (25%) and three parts roll to the flagstick (75%), use a 7-iron; if the edge of the green is half-way between you and the flagstick, use a 9-iron or pitching wedge; if you have three parts carry to the green (75%) and one part roll to the flagstick (25%), use a sand or lob wedge. Concentrate on landing the ball on the front of the green and letting it roll to the flagstick.

If you are faced with an uphill shot, you need to decrease the loft of the club you're chipping with, say from a 7-iron to a 6-iron or even a 5-iron. Conversely, if chipping downhill you'll need to increase the loft; for example, if you determine you would need a 7-iron on level ground, you might select an 8- or 9-iron to play to a downhill pin.

Similarly, if you are chipping to a green which features a landing area with a sidehill lie, be sure to account for some extra roll as the ball comes off the sidehill slope.

% Flight	% Roll	Club:
25%	75%	7-iron
50%	50%	9-iron or pitching wedge
75%	25%	sand wedge or lob wedge

29

BUMP & RUN

SET-UP

The basic stance is the same as with a short pitch: parallel shoulders, left foot withdrawn from the line to create an open foot alignment, but the stance narrows a bit. However, the **ball position** is just **at the midway point**. **70% of the body weight is** on the **left foot** and the **hands** are just **opposite the inside of the left thigh**. Depending of the length of the shot, **grip down** on the club. The set-up dictates the position at impact and ensures a slight downward contact on the ball.

MAKING THE SWING

The swing is a **rhythmic, pendulum-style** with very **passive wrists** and the **weight remaining on the left foot during the backswing**. The **length of the backswing is entirely related to the distance the ball has to travel**. It allows for a smoothly accelerating stroke to take place through the ball, achieving a similar length follow-through to backswing.

The swing is mainly with the hands and arms. On the follow through do not allow the clubhead to pass your hands. They should feel "soft" in making the shot.

7 IRON 25% FLIGHT / 75% ROLL

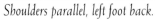

Shoulders parallel, left foot back. *With a 7-iron, a short backswing.*

9 IRON 50% FLIGHT / 50% ROLL

Hands inside left thigh. Ball in middle of stance. *With a 9-iron, a little longer.*

SAND WEDGE 75% FLIGHT / 25% ROLL

Narrowed stance. *With the sand wedge, the swing is even longer and more languid.*

Note how the finish mirrors the backswing.

On the follow-through, don't allow the clubhead to pass your hands.

The "short" finish.

The swing smoothly accelerates.

With a more lofted club, use a higher finish.

Weight finishes on the left side.

BASIC PITCH

The need to reduce the amount of power generated is paramount. The most common mistake with this shot is to swing too far back, then decelerate through the ball, creating all kinds of mis-hits.

Ball position the same as any full wedge shot—just left of the center of the stance.

It is very important to gauge the backswing length so that a smoothly accelerating swing will send the ball the correct distance.

SET-UP

The main factor at setup is that the position developed is consistent with the length of the swing used. **The width of the stance must be narrowed in relation to the reduced distance of shot** required. The shorter the shot, the narrower the stance. The **ball** will stay in its normal **position** for a wedge shot, **just left of the center of the stance**. The **shoulders remain parallel** to the ball-to-target line but the **left foot** should be **withdrawn slightly**, allowing the **foot alignment** to be **open**. This should be opened up little by little as the shot gets shorter, up to a maximum of approximately 30°. **Weight** should **favor** the **left side** on a **60/40 ratio**, keeping the hands ahead of the ball, with the left hand opposite the inside of the left thigh as usual. The feel is **soft and light**, so grip pressure should be a little more relaxed than for a full shot.

MAKING THE SHOT

The swing should feel like a mini version of a full shot. The rhythm must be smooth and no attempt should be made to use the wrists excessively. **Move everything away** from the ball **together**, let the **wrists set naturally**.

Keep everything together as the weight is moved back to the left side, and **release the club freely** through the ball.

At the end of the follow-through the weight should be mainly on the left foot, with the club travelling at least as far through as it was taken back. Good balance throughout is a sign that all is well.

Everything—hands, wrists, arms, legs and body—moves together, both back and through. The wrists set naturally.

The wrists set naturally.

Release the club freely.

Weight transfers freely to the left side.

Keep the clubface square to the target at address. Then **focus on making your normal swing**, hitting confidently through impact and **following through up along the slope**. Just so long as you accelerate the clubhead smoothly and at the same time keep your hands nice and soft, the ball should comfortably reach the green and settle quickly.

Keep club face square and follow the slope

THEORY

Whenever you're attempting to chip from a sloping lie, your first consideration should always be that the slope will either add to or subtract from the loft on the clubface.

UPHILL CHIP

Faced with an uphill slope, many golfers automatically reach for their sand wedge, thinking that it will help them get the ball up the slope. Big mistake. If you were to attempt this shot with your sand wedge, which itself has about 56 degrees of loft, on a slope of about 30 degrees, you're effectively playing with much more loft than a normal shot. That's way too much, so think about taking a less-lofted club, a 9-iron, say, or even an 8-iron to keep the ball a little lower to the ground and ensure that you get forward rather than upward momentum on the shot.

Using the sand wedge will produce much too much loft

The 8 or 9-iron will produce optimum loft

30° upward slope

The UPHILL CHIP

The cardinal error in this shot is underestimating the effects of the upslope and leaving the ball well short of the pin. In view of this, your club selection and whole set-up should be geared towards propelling the ball **forwards** rather than upwards off the turf. However, one of the drawbacks of being aggressive enough to get the ball up to the green is that you'll impart less backspin through impact and therefore you may find that the ball will run out considerably on landing. Once again, one of the keys to executing the shot proficiently is to set-up so that you can **swing with the slope**. Set **most of your weight on your right side** to anchor your swing and **lighten your grip** pressure a touch to "soften" the shot.

Ball back in stance.

Lighten grip a little to "soften" the shot

Most weight on right side

Follow-through up along the slope…

Chipping: The UPHILL CHIP

The slope shown is about 30 degrees. Faced with this kind of situation, many golfers automatically reach for their sand wedge, thinking that it will help them get the ball up the slope. Big mistake. If you were to attempt this shot with your sand wedge, which itself has about 56 degrees of loft, you're effectively playing with much more loft than on a level lie. That's way too much, so think about taking a less-lofted club; a 9-iron or even an 8-iron to keep the ball a little lower to the ground and ensure that you get forward rather than upward momentum on the shot.

30° upward slope

The slope shown is about 30 degrees, but in this case it's actually detracting from the loft on the clubface. Faced with this situation, many players try to caress the ball down the slope using something like a 5-iron. The loft on the standard 5-iron is somewhere between 28 and 30 degrees. Now take off the 30 degrees of the slope and you'll discover that you're actually playing with a club which has a negative amount of loft on the face. To "soften" the shot a little and to help get the ball airborne, opt for one of your most lofted clubs; the sand wedge, pitching wedge or lob wedge.

(While I prefer to play the ball somewhat forward, many play the ball a bit farther back in the stance to ensure a crisp, firm hit.)

30° downward slope

Chipping:
The DOWNHILL CHIP

KEYS TO CHIPPING ON UNEVEN LIES:

1. *Weight on the lower foot*
2. *Soften your grip*
3. *Swing with or along the slope*

DOWNHILL CHIP

When playing on a downward slope, the slope itself is detracting from the loft on the clubface. Faced with this situation, many players try to caress the ball down the slope using something like a 5-iron. The loft on the standard 5-iron is somewhere between 28 and 30 degrees. Now take off the 30 degrees of the slope and you'll discover that you're actually playing with a club which has a negative amount of loft on the face. Clubs of choice should be the sand wedge, pitching wedge or lob wedge.

The sand, pitching or lob wedge will produce optimum loft

30° downward slope

Using a 5 iron will actually produce negative loft and far too much topspin

Once you've understood the principle of taking a more lofted club to negate the effects of the downslope, your next step is to adopt an address position which will allow you to **swing with the slope** rather than fight against it. In this case it means setting **the majority of your weight on your left side**. If you open up the clubface quite dramatically to get some extra loft on the face, compensate for this by aiming a little left of

Although I like to play the ball forward on a downhill chip, you may want to move it back a wee bit so as to ensure solid contact.

Play the ball forward

Majority of weight on left side

Take the or slight

Swing with the slope…

The DOWNHILL CHIP

the target and choking down on the grip for some extra control.

Playing the ball a little forward of the center of your stance, make sure that you take the club away straight back away from the ball or even fractionally outside the line. When you make your swing **the clubhead traces the contours of the ground rather than fights against them**. Some players see this as a "wristy" kind of shot, but for most players it's safer—not to mention easier—if you **keep your hands out of it**. Try to keep your wrists as passive as possible and feel as though you simply slide the clubface right under the ball. The ball should come off the clubface fairly softly and stop relatively quickly once it hits the green, despite the fact that you're playing downhill. Trust the loft on the clubface and don't try to scoop the ball up into the air.

club straight back
y outside of the line

Keep your wrists passive and "soften" your grip

Feel like you're sliding the club face under the ball, but allow the clubface to close naturally.

39

HIGH LOB

This shot is required when playing to a tight pin position with very little green to work with.

SET-UP

To achieve more height on a shot, more loft needs to be produced on the club at impact. This is one of the keys to effectively hitting the high lob shot. The easiest way of doing this is to **open the face of the club at set-up** and keep it open throughout the shot. This must be done before the grip is established on the club.

Move the ball as far forward in the stance as the lie will permit. This places the hands level with, or even behind, the ball and **sets the majority of your weight (60%) on the right foot**. Returning through this position at impact will guarantee that the shot will fly more up than forward, producing a very high, soft landing shot.

Hands even with or slightly behind the ball.

Note that the stance is open relative to the projected flight of the ball.

Weight back.

Clubface open.

Ball forward.

MAKING THE SHOT

The swing for a high lob shot is basically a soft one made in what feels like slow motion (one-half to three-quarter speed). The arm swing is gentle with a small amount of leg action.

From a ball position that is forward in your stance, (5) **return the club to the same open position as at address**. (1) **The back-swing is amazingly long for such a short shot**. You need to feel that you are literally (5) **sliding the club face under the ball through impact** to an (8) abbreviated finish.

(7) The result is a very high, soft landing shot that will roll a short way on the green from left to right once it lands.

Hold the clubface open through impact.

Hold the club-face open on the way back, through impact and to the finish.

Picture a slower, rhythmical pace to the swing.

Note how high the ball flies.

Feel like you are sliding the clubface under the ball.

A good image to concentrate on is keeping the face of the club pointing towards the sky at the finish of the shot.

1/2 SAND WEDGE

This shot is used many times after laying-up from a position where it was wholly unrealistic to reach the green—whether from a fairway bunker, the rough or perhaps some gorse. The key to the 1/2 sand wedge is laying-up a sufficient distance from the green to be able to play an aggressive shot. You need to pick both the appropriate distance <u>and</u> the side of the fairway where you wish to attack the flagstick. The ideal distance to be able to play this shot is 40 to 70 yards from the flagstick.

SET-UP

Use a **normal width stance, slightly open** to the intended line of flight, and a normal grip. As you get closer to the green, the stance narrows and it is best to choke down a bit on the grip.

MAKING THE SHOT

From 70 or 80 yards out, **make an aggressive, well-balanced swing** with a 3/4 backswing to a 3/4 follow-through. From 40 to 50 yards out, use a 1/2 backswing to an abbreviated follow-through. Try to **carry the ball back to the hole** or slightly beyond, to allow the ball to spin back close to the hole once it hits the green.

Playing
in the
Elements

*A wet Ian Woosnan battles the elements
in the 1992 Open at Muirfield.*

Playing in the Wind

INTO THE WIND

Wind is always stronger on links courses because they are close to the sea and there are very few trees. Always factor in windy elements when playing links courses.

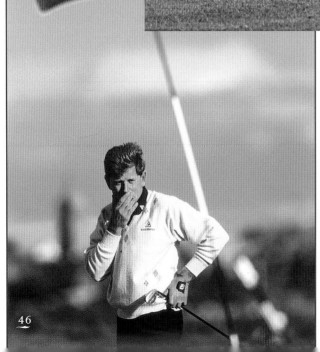

Nick Price battles windy conditions at the 1995 Open championship at St. Andrews.

SET-UP

Widen your stance and play the **ball a bit back** of the normal position. **Sit a little at address** to lower your center of gravity.

Low and slow is the watchword on the backswing.

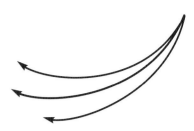

The wind on links courses…

A good, wide takeaway.

Arms in front of chest. Good right knee flex throughout.

Stay down and follow through. A longer, lower follow through will tend to produce a lower trajectory. A slow pace to the entire swing is paramount.

Always take 1-2 clubs more and **swing slower**—surprisingly this decreases backspin and hits the ball lower. The **first two feet of the swing** are very important—keep it **low and slow** to avoid a steep angle of attack and backspin on the ball.

Playing in the Wind
DOWNWIND

Set up as with any full shot, but with the ball somewhat forward in your stance. Concentrate on making a full turn back.

Make a well-balanced swing and hit the ball slightly harder, which will result in the ball going higher. **Use less club** than you normally would as the ball will carry a lot further and will land with very little or no backspin.

Play the ball a little forward in your stance to hit it higher.

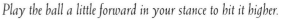

Make a well balanced swing.

Hit a little harder than usual.

Concentrating on a good, full finish will help you hit the ball a bit harder.

Playing in the Wind
CROSS WIND

Wind direction ⬅--------- ⬅-------- ⬅

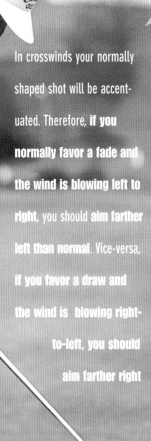

In crosswinds your normally shaped shot will be accentuated. Therefore, **if you normally favor a fade and the wind is blowing left to right,** you should **aim farther left than normal.** Vice-versa, **if you favor a draw and the wind is blowing right-to-left, you should aim farther right** **than normal.** Although my normal shot is a left-to-right fade, I'm hitting a draw here with a right-to-left crosswind.

Alternately, you can try to negate the wind by playing a fade into a right-to-left wind (or a draw against a left-to-right wind) to hold your shot against the wind. This shot is much trickier, but the reward is that it will land much softer.

LOW PUNCH WEDGE

This is one of the most
desirable and useful
shots to have in your
shot-making arsenal when
you need to hit a shot that
bores through the windy
conditions typically
encountered on a links.

This is the one which,
especially when played
with a balata covered ball,
comes onto the green
loaded with backspin.
Because it is typically
played into the wind, it can
really back-up once it hits.

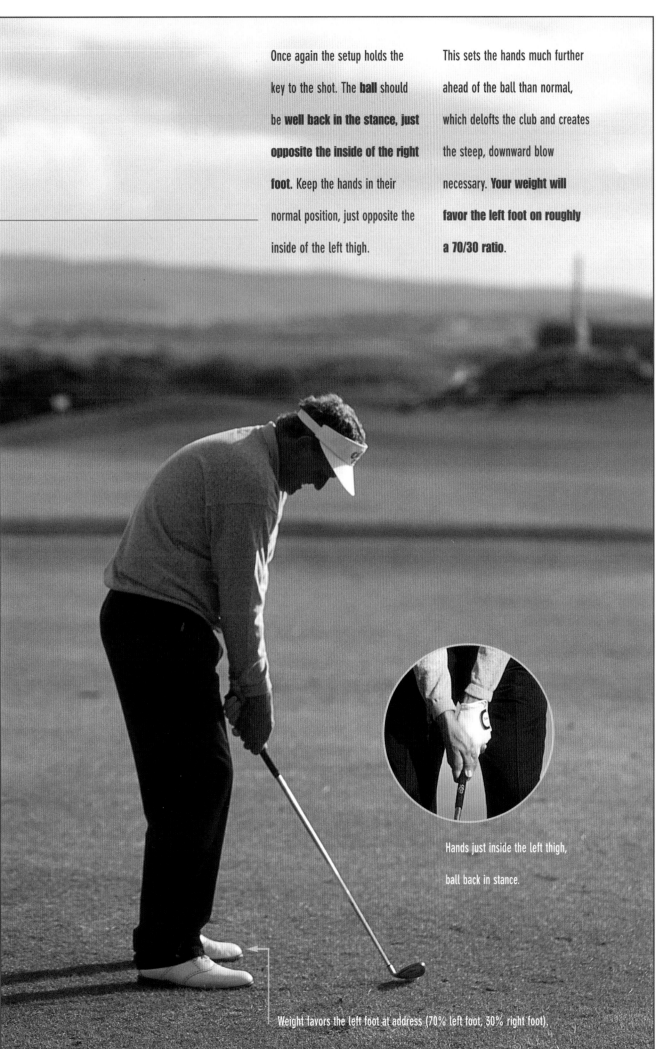

SET-UP

Once again the setup holds the key to the shot. The **ball** should be **well back in the stance, just opposite the inside of the right foot.** Keep the hands in their normal position, just opposite the inside of the left thigh.

This sets the hands much further ahead of the ball than normal, which delofts the club and creates the steep, downward blow necessary. **Your weight will favor the left foot on roughly a 70/30 ratio.**

Hands just inside the left thigh, ball back in stance.

Weight favors the left foot at address (70% left foot, 30% right foot).

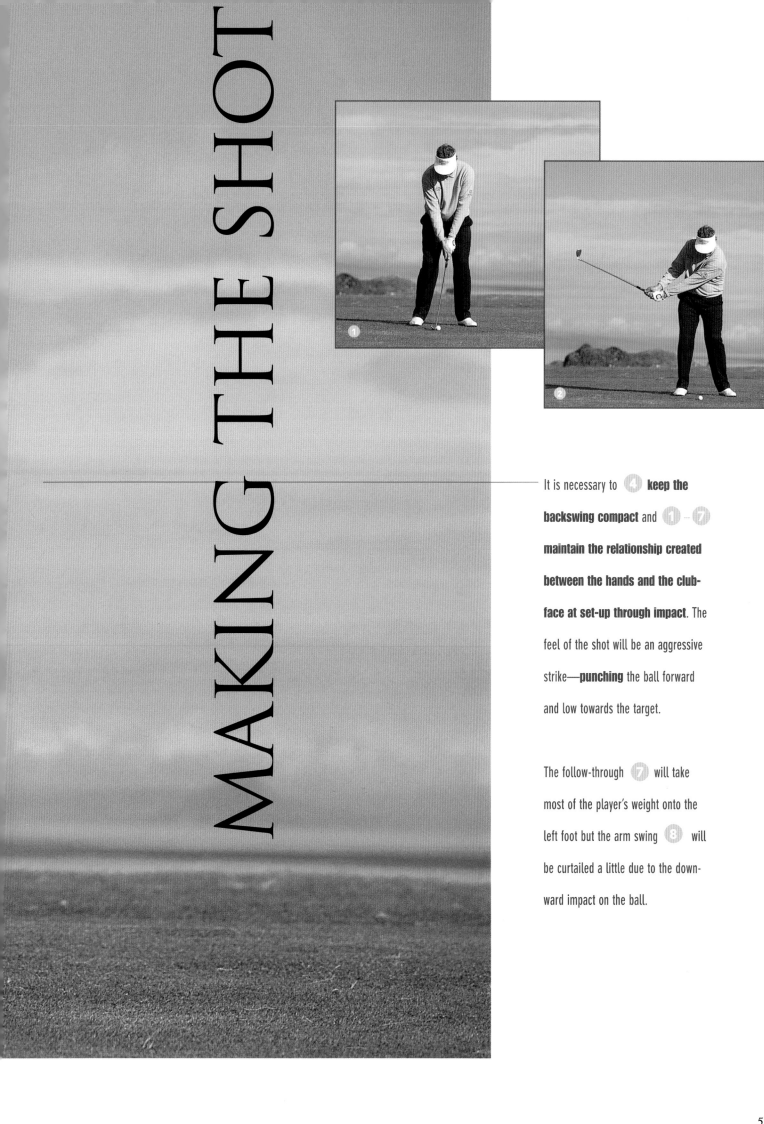

MAKING THE SHOT

It is necessary to (4) **keep the backswing compact** and (1) – (7) **maintain the relationship created between the hands and the club-face at set-up through impact**. The feel of the shot will be an aggressive strike—**punching** the ball forward and low towards the target.

The follow-through (7) will take most of the player's weight onto the left foot but the arm swing (8) will be curtailed a little due to the downward impact on the ball.

Note the abbreviated, compact backswing and **5** **6** the firm left side just before and after impact.

Be aggressive! Feel like you're punching the ball through impact.

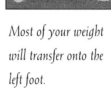

Most of your weight will transfer onto the left foot.

Note the truncated follow-through and the well-balanced finish.

Is Your
5-IRON...
A 210-Yard or a 120-Yard Club?

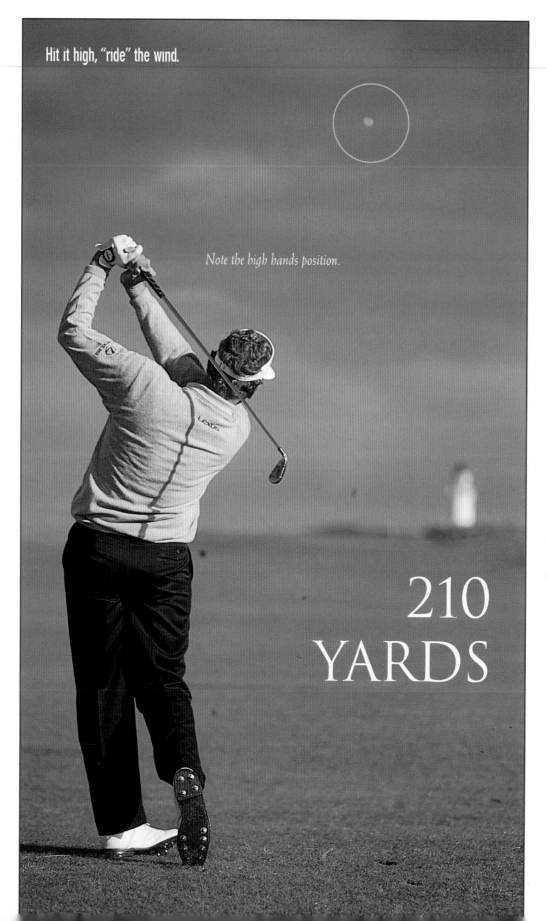

Hit it high, "ride" the wind.

Note the high hands position.

210 YARDS

Downwind

When playing downwind your 5-iron will reach optimum height then start to gradually fall to the ground. When it hits the ground, it will have little or no backspin on in, depending on the severity of the wind and how hard the ground is.

When playing downwind, play the ball a bit forward of the usual position and take a full swing, finishing with hands high. Don't be afraid to use the wind to gain extra distance.

Into the Wind

Into the wind, the ball will climb to its optimum height and then fall almost vertically and will not run very far when it lands. Into a strong wind the ball sometimes looks as though it is coming back to you.

When playing into the wind, keep the club low and slow to the ground on your backswing. If you pick the club up too quickly, it promotes a wristy steep swing which creates a steep angle of attack and a lot of spin; spin makes the ball climb into the wind. Take plenty of club and swing the club smoothly with rhythm; the harder you swing the more spin you put on the ball. Use a somewhat restricted backswing and finish with your hands shoulder high.

Hit it low, "under" the wind.

Note the more "rounded" finish.

120 YARDS

Playing in the Wind
PUTTING

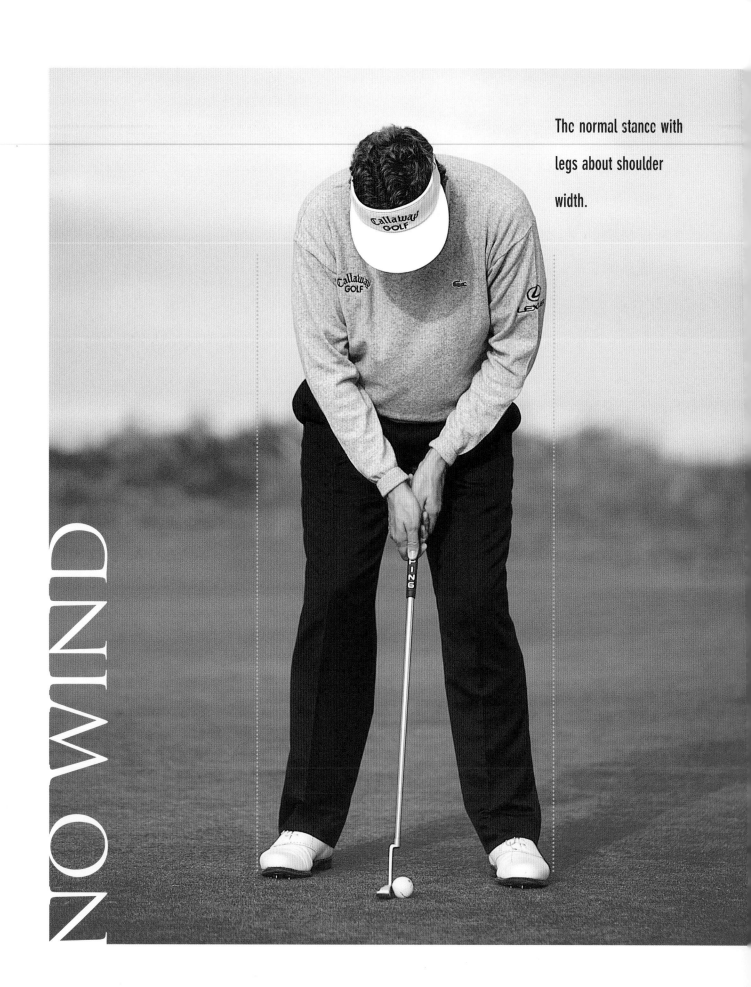

The normal stance with legs about shoulder width.

NO WIND

When it is particularly windy, it is helpful to widen your stance to remain balanced over the ball.

At address, do not ground your putter because if the ball moves due to the wind, you incur a one-stroke penalty. At address just hover your putter above the ground.

Grip down.

The Hovering Club...

WIND

RAIN

Playing in the rain is difficult on any type of course, but it is made worse on links courses because of the wind.

When it starts to rain, and looks like it will continue, **put on your rainsuit as soon as possible**.

Remember to **grip the club slightly tighter** than normal, **swing slower** and **take one more club** than usual.

In the rain the playing surface tends to get much "heavier." Pitches tend to come up short as the ball won't spin or roll as much.

And always keep a dry towel in your bag and at least one extra glove.

Awkward Lies

On a links course you are more likely to be confronted with an awkward lie even if you are in the middle of the fairway. This is due to the undulating fairways on links courses. Therefore, you should be prepared to face a number of shots from awkward lies.

Justin Leonard pitches out from an extremely awkward lie next to the bunker fronting the 17th hole at the 1999 Open championship at Carnoustie.

BARE LIE

Because of the sometimes
"scruffy" nature of some areas
around a links, occasionally one
will encounter the ball lying
in an area where there is
very little turf. Playing
off of a bare lie entails a
little different technique.

*Grip down a little.
Hands somewhat forward*

*Center
of stance.*

Ball back

MAKING THE SHOT

Stay down through the shot and aggressively take a divot in front of the ball.

Ball first, turf second. Note the divot ahead of the original ball position.

Hands a bit forward, grip down on the club slightly and **play the ball back in your stance**. It is very important to **hit the ball first**, and **turf second**.

The tendency here is to look up too quickly to see where the ball has gone. This results in a thinned shot.

61

MAKING THE SHOT

④ ⑤ ⑥ The club is swung along the body line as normal and the shot is **played ① - ⑦ mostly with the hands and arms**.

While it is important to make an inside move from the top of the backswing, be careful that it is not too much so. Concentrate on coming down the line of aim through the hitting area.

With the ball above your feet, **concentrate on making a high-hands finish**. If you were to make a more rounded swing, with hands ending shoulder high, the shot will draw far too much.

Note the initial flight of the ball is to the right of the target. Trust that; if struck properly, it will detour back to the flagstick.

A nice high finish, not around the body.

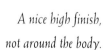

Ball ABOVE FEET

Grip down on the shaft slightly.

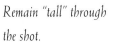

Remain "tall" through the shot.

Maintain good knee flex.

As a result of the hooking flight and a general tendency to pull the shot, **(1) the clubface is aimed to the right**, the amount being determined by the severity of the slope.

The grip will be the same except that the player moves down the shaft because the ball is closer to the hands.

(2) Feet, hips and shoulders are aligned with the clubhead so that both body and clubhead are pointing in the same direction.

(1) (2) The ball is in the center of the stance.

Full Shots:
Ball ABOVE FEET

"A Hook Lie"

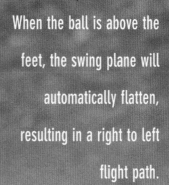

When the ball is above the feet, the swing plane will automatically flatten, resulting in a right to left flight path.

Full Shots:
Ball BELOW FEET

"A Slice Lie"

When the ball is below the feet, the swing plane is forced to become more upright, and the ball will travel from left to right.

MAKING THE SHOT

It is important to "measure down to the ball" with a good knee flex. Keeping good balance is vital with the ball lying below your feet. Therefore, focus on keeping most of your weight toward your heels throughout the shot.

Make a regular swing, being careful to **remain balanced**. Play the shot mainly with the hands and arms to help maintain balance.

5 **6** Concentrate on making a good inside move from the top of your backswing so as not to come over the top. Try to hit it from the inside, and think of making a smooth swing.

Good knee flex throughout helps you get down to the ball.

Since there is a tendency to lose your balance in this type of shot, try to keep your weight slightly "heelward" through the shot.

Ball BELOW FEET

The club is held at its full length.

With the ball below your feet, the swing plane is forced to become more upright. Subsequently, the ball will travel from left to right.

1 **The blade is aimed to the left** to allow for the slicing flight, the amount being determined by the severity of the slope.

Whereas in 'ball above the feet' the club can be made shorter; on this shot the club cannot be made longer, and so **the club is held at its full length**. Therefore, the **knees are flexed more than** **normal** to help the player 'get down' to the ball. **Alignment is in keeping with the aim of the blade**.

The stance is assumed as normal until the player's balance is affected by the slope and the appropriate action is taken to maintain balance.

Full Shots:
The UPHILL LIE

With an uphill lie, more club is needed than normal, dependent on the slope, as the ball will fly higher.

More weight on the lower foot

SET-UP

The blade is aimed to the right as the ball will draw in flight. This is because the legs will be restricted in the follow–through and the hands will take over and close the blade. The steeper the slope, the more this will happen and, therefore, the severity of the slope will determine how far to the right one aims. Concentrate on a smooth weight transfer; often a pull is more likely than a draw since weight is difficult to transfer through the shot.

When playing off level ground the body is virtually perpendicular to the ground. On sloping ground this is no longer the case. Therefore, stand to the ball so your shoulders are parallel to the slope. To achieve this, **more weight is placed on the lower foot** (the steepness of the slope will determine how much).

The feet, hips and shoulders are aligned perpendicular to the clubface as the amount of hook spin has already been determined by the aim of the blade. This will mean that both club and body will still be aligned.

Note: The clubface turns over more quickly than usual due to less leg action, although this is difficult to see in still photographs.

The ball is positioned nearer the high foot to encourage the clubhead to follow the contour of the slope. However, many players prefer to position the ball to the center of the stance, since there is a tendency to get "stuck" by gravity on the back foot.

NOTE: With both an uphill and downhill lie, more weight is applied to the lower foot.

MAKING THE SHOT

Once you've set-up properly, make a full normal swing. It will be difficult to have a full free follow-through, as gravity and the upslope will restrict foot and leg action.

Full Shots:
The DOWNHILL LIE

Less club is taken as the club will be delofted as it follows the contour.

Ball is played toward the middle of the stance.

More weight on lower foot.

Blade and body aimed left of the intended target.

SET-UP

The blade is aimed to the left as the ball will cut or slice in flight. This is because the contour of the slope will force the club to be swung on a more upright plane. The severity of the slope will determine how much.

As with the uphill shot, **more weight is applied to the lower foot** to achieve the perpendicular effect. Again the amount is determined by the severity of the slope. **Feet, hips and shoulders are aligned perpendicular** to the blade as the amount of slice spin has already been decided by the aim of the blade. This means **club and body** will still be **aligned together**. **The ball is positioned nearer the high foot** to encourage the club-head to follow the contour of the slope.

MAKING THE SHOT

The club is swung in the normal way but the legs must remain fully flexed throughout the swing. Aim slightly left and swing with the slope.

NOTE:

With both a downhill and uphill lie, more weight is applied to the lower foot.

Maintain flex throughout.

Thick
ROUGH

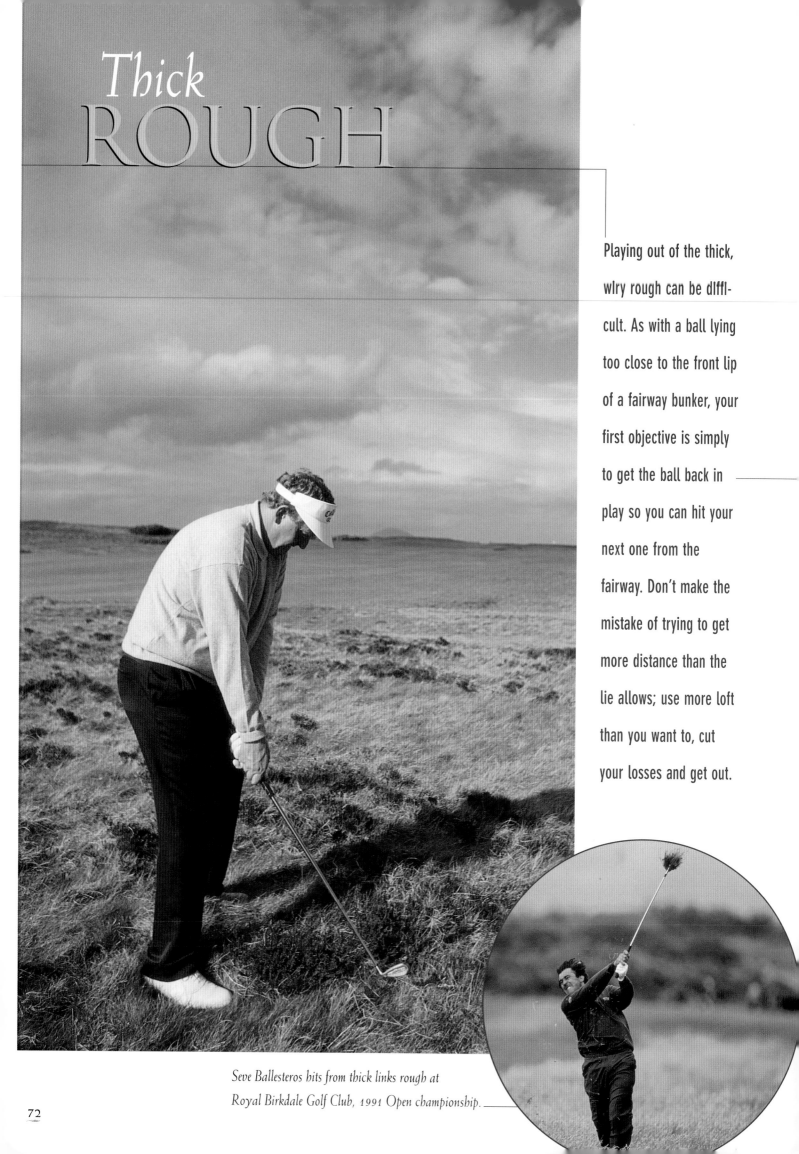

Playing out of the thick, wiry rough can be diffi-cult. As with a ball lying too close to the front lip of a fairway bunker, your first objective is simply to get the ball back in play so you can hit your next one from the fairway. Don't make the mistake of trying to get more distance than the lie allows; use more loft than you want to, cut your losses and get out.

Seve Ballesteros hits from thick links rough at Royal Birkdale Golf Club, 1991 Open championship.

Open your stance relative to the ball-target line. **Place the ball in the center** of your stance with **70%** of your **weight** on the **left foot**.

Align the clubface to the right of the intended target because, when the club approaches the ball, the long grass may catch the hosel first and close the face, sending the ball further left than you expect. **Hold the club a little firmer** than usual to stop it from twisting in your hands.

SET-UP

Stay down.

MAKING THE SHOT

Swing the club along the line of your feet. Hit into the back of the ball **with a descending blow**; it is very important to **follow through** as much as the thick grass will allow.

Keep your eye on the ball, if you can see it!

Notice the extension of the arms and the weight totally released onto the left leg for a powerful descending blow.

Reading UNDULATING GREENS

Choose an intermediate target between yourself and the hole and "feel" how fast you want the ball to be rolling when it passes over the target. Getting the pace of the putt correct is more important on long putts than the line.

The key to putting on undulating greens is to concentrate on putting to an imaginary target on the line you've picked out. Then concentrate on making a swing with the proper effort to get the ball to the hole.

MAKING THE SHOT

Imaginary hole.

For the ball to take the break **it must be travelling at the correct speed**. When lining up to putt with a big break it is useful to ① ② ③ **use an imaginary hole to aim at**, since it is often difficult to convince yourself to allow enough break on the green. If you have a good caddie, take his advice; remember, he has probably seen the putt before.

If you are **unsure of the line on a breaking putt, give it a little extra on the high side of the hole**; it's not called the "professionals' side" for nothing.

On a links course you will also have to **consider the wind direction** because this will affect the putt dramatically.

Remember, your goal is to two putt—no more.

TIPS...

PUTTING

Contrary to what you might think when you see the top players rolling the ball into the hole from all over the place, you don't have to be an exceptionally gifted golfer to be a good putter. While it requires skill, hand-eye coordination and strength to hit a 3-iron stone dead from 200 yards out, you don't really need these attributes to read greens and judge distance, the two main keys for consistent putting.

Good putting is all about confidence and feel. If you have those two factors in abundance, you're going to hole a lot of putts, no question. And remember what they say: "A good putter is a match for anyone."

If in doubt, hit the ball straight at the hole

Don't fall into the trap of looking for breaks that aren't there. Trust your instinct. If you can't see an obvious break, chances are there isn't one. And even if there is, it's only going to be subtle.

On a putt of under 10 to 15 feet or so on most traditional British greens, if you hit the ball firm and straight, you've got a great chance of holing it, even if the ball drifts off line by a couple of inches.

Distance is more important than line

When you're putting, how many times do you miss the hole by five or six feet to the left or right, even from long range? Probably not that many. How many times do you leave the ball at least four, five or six feet short of the hole, even on shortish length putts? Probably an awful lot more.

That simple statistic reveals one very important piece of information—that you can already read the break on putts fairly well. If that's the case, forget about spending ages studying the line of your putts and instead concentrate your efforts on accurately judging the pace and distance.

If you can get the ball up to the hole regularly, you're going to leave yourself a lot of tap-in pars. And if you become competent at judging distance, you'll be amazed at how well you'll be able to spot the line and how many of those birdie putts become makeable.

Hit your putts on the upswing

One of the keys to successful putting is imparting topspin onto the ball during the stroke, so that it accelerates off the putter face at impact and holds its line as it rolls towards the hole. The best way of doing this is to make contact with the ball slightly on the upswing, allowing the upward brushing motion of the putter face to do all the work. That's one of my key putting thoughts.

Don't feel as though you have to play the ball forward in your stance to do this. As you can see from the above photo, I have the ball positioned just about in the middle of my stance. From here, once I've taken the putter away low to the ground in my backswing, I simply concentrate on making a gentle upward sweeping motion as I swing the putter through towards the hole.

Don't exaggerate this movement too much, though, as you'll risk hitting the ball with the sole or bottom edge of your putter, or missing it completely. The key to imparting topspin while maintaining the quality of strike is to keep this movement gentle. Once you get it right, you'll find that your putts will start to reach the hole more convincingly and hold their line better, too.

Bunker Play

Tiger Woods blasts out of the sand at the 8th hole at the 1998 Open championship at Royal Birkdale.

FAIRWAY BUNKERS
"Just Get It Out"

When you have a high front bunker face and can't reach the green

If you can't get your shot safely out of the bunker and onto the green, your first priority is to just get it out and back onto the fairway. Sometimes you will just have to take what the shot gives you and play out sideways or even backward.

SET-UP

Hands are back, perhaps even behind the ball.

60% of your weight is on the back foot.

Ball is forward.

Play the ball forward in your stance with your hands even with or slightly behind the ball. Weight distribution should favor the back foot.

Hold the clubface open through impact.

MAKING THE SHOT

Concentrate on getting the ball back in play.

Don't be afraid of being aggressive.

Bunker Play
FAIRWAY BUNKERS

When you have enough room to clear the bunker's front lip

SET-UP

It is vital to take a sufficiently lofted club to clear the bunker wall.

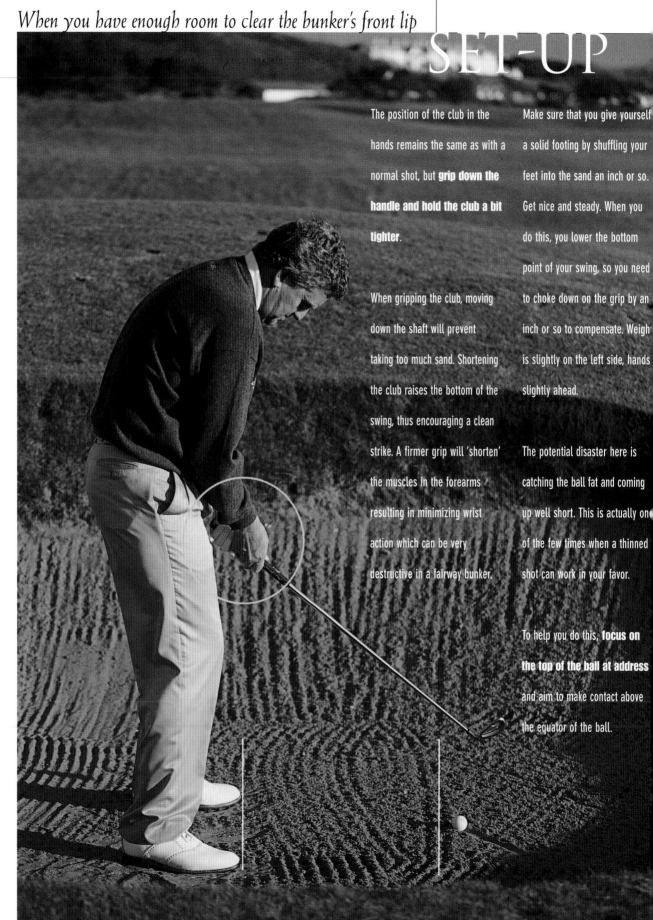

The position of the club in the hands remains the same as with a normal shot, but **grip down the handle and hold the club a bit tighter**.

When gripping the club, moving down the shaft will prevent taking too much sand. Shortening the club raises the bottom of the swing, thus encouraging a clean strike. A firmer grip will 'shorten' the muscles in the forearms resulting in minimizing wrist action which can be very destructive in a fairway bunker.

Make sure that you give yourself a solid footing by shuffling your feet into the sand an inch or so. Get nice and steady. When you do this, you lower the bottom point of your swing, so you need to choke down on the grip by an inch or so to compensate. Weight is slightly on the left side, hands slightly ahead.

The potential disaster here is catching the ball fat and coming up well short. This is actually one of the few times when a thinned shot can work in your favor.

To help you do this, **focus on the top of the ball at address** and aim to make contact above the equator of the ball.

The stance adopted is the same as normal but the feet are very slightly lowered into the sand. This give a firm foundation and prevents slipping. However, the feet must not be dug in excessively. Align the body normally, with feet, hips and shoulders parallel to the ball-to-target line.

MAKING THE SHOT

Maintain height.

1 2 The **ball should be placed slightly nearer to the left heel** to encourage the player to hit the ball slightly on the upswing. Swing nice and slow for the first few feet. **4 5** Try to pick it cleanly off the sand with solid contact.

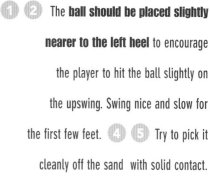

Try to keep at a consistent height and level hips throughout.

 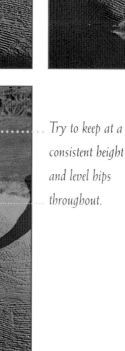 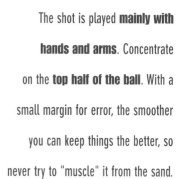

It's important to stay down through the shot. Concentrate on the top of the ball.

The shot is played **mainly with hands and arms**. Concentrate on the **top half of the ball**. With a small margin for error, the smoother you can keep things the better, so never try to "muscle" it from the sand.

GREENSIDE BUNKERS

Once the ball hits the green, "slice" sidespin will carry it from left-to-right towards the hole

Set-up left of the flag stick.

The Splash Shot

This is the basic greenside bunker shot with the ball lying well in good sand, and the pin some 10–20 yards away. It is a very similar shot to the high lob wedge shot, but played from sand instead of grass. Most greenside bunkers will have a lip to get over and the shot will, therefore, need to get up into the air quickly. This will have to be taken into consideration at set-up.

SET-UP

The aim, stance and alignment are adjusted to the left of the intended target. This sets the **clubface** open to the stance and body alignment but **square to the ball-to-target line.**

The **ball position is well forward in the stance**—opposite the left heel and left instep—helping create the early lift required to get over the lip. This places the ball some **two to three inches ahead of the normal strike point** with an iron, encouraging the player to strike the sand before the ball and build up the cushion of sand essential for a good greenside bunker shot.

The posture remains the same with the exception that the **feet should be wriggled into the sand until the soles of the shoes have just been covered.**

A shot from the sand should present no more of a problem than a chip from off the edge of the green or a long range putt. A high level of confidence stems from a clear understanding of how to play the shot competently.

One thing you can't afford to get wrong is your address position. When you're playing out of a bunker, you're looking to **cut across the ball at impact**, so you need to set up open, with your **feet, hips and shoulders all aiming left of the target**. That way, when you make your normal swing back along the line of your feet, you'll automatically cut across the ball/target line through impact.

Another factor which contributes to consistent bunker play is your weight distribution. If you play the ball off your left instep and have approximately **85 to 90% of your weight on the left side**, it helps you pick the club up slightly in the back-swing and promotes a steeper and more positive attack into the ball.

Feet, hips and shoulders left of the target.

Feet wriggled into the sand.

Strike point in sand.

Direction to flag stick.

Ball forward.

MAKING THE SHOT

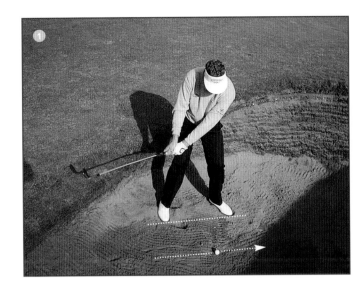

2 Concentrate on the sand where the club has to strike, rather than on the ball itself, 1 **swing the club on line with the stance and alignment**, striking the sand at the pre-determined point and **aggressively following-through**. You will need to concentrate on keeping the face open through impact, as in a high lob wedge from grass, by imagining that the face of the club is pointing to the sky throughout the follow-through.

2 5 The swing must be accurate, **hitting the sand the distance behind the ball which was pre-determined at set-up**.

Bunkers, by nature, are defined as hazards, so it should go without saying that your **number one priority** anytime you find your ball lying in one is to **escape successfully the first time**. No fancy swings, no attempts at delicate little splashes. Make sure you give the ball a good hard clump and get it out. Commitment is your biggest ally. If you can trust yourself to make at least a three-

quarter length swing every time from a slightly open stance and then **accelerate through impact**, the ball will come out each and every time. Once you're confident in getting out first time, every time, then you can refine your technique.

Under tournament conditions, though, safety first is your priority. Most regular bunker shots can be played with the lob wedge. The extra loft on the clubface enables you to make a confident, authoritative swing, safe in the knowledge that you can't hit the ball too far.

The swing for a normal greenside bunker shot is actually a little outside-in, thus imparting a bit of "slice" sidespin.

The stance is open, relative to the intended flight of the ball, and the length of the backswing varies with the distance to the flag stick.

Hit the pre-selected spot behind the ball and aggressively follow through.

Note the abbreviated follow-through and good knee flex throughout the swing.

Greenside Bunkers
PLUGGED LIE

A badly plugged ball in a bunker strikes fear in the best of us. At first glance, it appears to be one of the most difficult shots in all of golf, especially for the amateur. With proper execution and confidence, it need not be.

Concentrate on a spot about an inch behind the ball.

Play the ball in the middle of your stance with a square or slightly closed clubface.

The key to effectively extricating yourself from a plugged lie is to utilize the leading edge of the sand iron. To do so, **the clubface has to be square or even slightly closed**. There is no need to alter the aim or alignment if the face is square. If it is slightly closed you will need to aim a little to the right of the intended target.

The main change at setup comes in the **ball position** which is **farther back in the stance, opposite the middle of the feet**.

Keeping the hands in their normal position—just opposite the inside of the left thigh—means they are considerably farther ahead of the ball than in a normal shot. Coupled with **more weight—up to 70%—being placed on the left foot**, allows you to create the steeply descending blow necessary to play this shot successfully. Like the splash shot, it is important to **wriggle the feet into the sand, perhaps to an even larger extent than for the ordinary sand shot**.

With a plugged lie it is essential to use the leading edge of the sand wedge to sharply enter the sand behind the ball and reach the bottom of the ball. With a "fried egg" lie, hit down sharply at the edge of the "egg white" and concentrate on driving the club into the sand.

Note

An early wrist break is essential.

The swing must create a steep angle of attack to help the player strike down into the sand. The player must ① **look at the sand one to two inches behind the ball**, and **not at the ball itself**.

There must be ② **an early wrist break in the backswing** to create the steep angle of attack and a ④ good strike down into the sand is essential. ⑥ There will be little or no follow-through with this shot as the sand will absorb all the energy of the swing. This is not a problem; ⑤ just **accelerate the club into the sand one to two inches behind the ball** and the ball will pop out of the plugged lie.

steep angle of attack...

Note the steep
angle of attack.

Aggressively strike
a point just behind
the ball.

The nature of this shot will not

produce any backspin on the

ball and so allowance will have

to be made for the ball running

a considerable distance after it

lands on the green.

COURSE STRATEGY

Your opening tee shot sets the tone for the day—choose your favorite club.

There's no written rule which states that you have to use your driver on the first tee, but time after time I see amateurs automatically reach for that club, knowing that they've little or no chance of hitting it well. Your opening tee shot sets the tone for the day, so if you're not confident hitting a wood, select your favorite club instead—I'm lucky, mine's the driver. It's far better to hit your 7-iron 150 yards down the middle of the fairway than your driver 200 yards in the heather or gorse, where you'll feel dejected and angry with yourself. There's plenty of time later in the round for more aggressive plays off the tee.

If you find that your favorite club is a 3-iron, consider using it to tee-off with and thus build confidence off the first tee. Remember to aim to the side of the fairway that favors your particular swing pattern; it enlarges the target area considerably.

Aim for one side of the fairway.

It's often said that the straight shot is the hardest shot in golf to play. It also gives you the least margin for error. If you aim straight, you are only really aiming for half of the fairway as the ball can go left or right. Take me, for example. I like to play a slight fade off the tee, which means I can set up on the right side, aim down the left and cut the ball back into the fairway. That way I have 100 percent of the fairway to aim at. If my shot comes off as planned, I'll end up in the middle of the fairway, if I overdo it slightly it'll be right center and if I slice it too much, I'll probably still be on the right edge of the fairway or, at worst, in the semi rough. And vice-versa if you have a draw, then set up on the left side, aim down the right and find the middle of the fairway, or at the worst the left semi-rough.

The motto is to play with your stock shot, not fight against it.

Par 3 and approach shot strategy

Aim at one side of the green and therefore if you favor a fade or a draw, you make sure you avoid the hazards. Distance control is a vital aspect of any golf shot whether driving, iron play, chipping or putting. It is especially so on par 3 holes. To improve your

distance control, you should work on a repetitive swing and make sure that you always take enough club to reach the green. Too many amateurs finish short on par 3's; therefore take more club than you would imagine.

Eliminate your disaster shot

If you're a low handicapper, chances are your good shots are just as good as mine. Where we differ, though, is in our consistency. Your bad shot may be a high slice, while mine is a gentle push. Your bad shot might put you in the trees, mine will leave me on the right edge of the fairway or in the semi-rough. Your key to improving further is to identify your problem shot and then find a way of reducing its destructibility.

Allow for your mis-hit

Nobody, not even a top player, strikes the ball perfectly every time, so if you're a newcomer to the game, you have to expect to mis-hit the ball more often than not. My philosophy is that you should allow for your mis-hits by taking an extra club. That's smart course management and will allow you to "squeeze" the best possible score from your game.

Play the percentages when you stray from the fairway

It's a fact of life that, no matter how accurate you are off the tee, you're going to land in the rough every now and then. The key to keeping your

score ticking along, though, is not to allow one errant shot to lead to another. My philosophy is, if you can't safely find the green with your next shot, to make your worst score a bogey. By that I mean you should play safe and make sure that you have an opportunity to reach the green with your third shot. The worst thing you can possibly do is panic and attempt a miraculous recovery which even Seve Ballesteros wouldn't contemplate in his wildest dreams.

Carefully weigh your options. If you realistically believe you can reach the green with your second shot and there's plenty of margin for error if the shot doesn't come off as planned, it may be worth having a go; but if reaching the green is out of the question and there are plenty more hazards lurking around, it's just not worth it.

Don't be afraid to compile a good score

Does this scenario sound familiar? You're putting together a great round. You're swinging well, have a great touch on the greens and feel in complete control of just about every part of your game. Then you look at your scorecard, discover that you're three shots under your handicap with just a few holes to go and for some inexplicable reason start to play defensively. You back-off with the driver, get a little too cautious with your iron play and try to lag your putts instead of going for the hole. All of a sudden, your run of good scoring abruptly comes to an end and you start giving shots back to the course. I know all about that because I've been there myself.

The best piece of advice I can offer here is that whenever you find yourself in this situation, never try to protect your score. Simply carry on doing what has worked for you throughout your round. If you're hitting your driver well, don't switch to an iron off the tee for no reason. Likewise, if the hole looks as big as a bucket, capitalize on it. Days when everything goes right don't come along very often, so make the most of them when they arise and don't be afraid to score well.

Bogeys and double-bogeys

Bogeys add up slowly, but doubles add up very quickly. If you find trouble, make sure you drop just one shot.

Always take care of your equipment

Make sure you regularly clean your golf clubs. One of the most common questions that I get asked is "how do professionals get so much backspin?" One of the main reasons professionals generate backspin, is that their clubs, and especially their groves, are always *very* clean.

Clean your grips as well as your clubs, and change your grips when they start to become worn.

Make sure that your clubs have the correct lies, lofts and shafts—ask your professional to check all your clubs and to correct them if necessary. A good pair of golf shoes is vital—your stance and anchor to the playing surface is a vital component of the golf swing. Also, with soft spikes so prevalent today, be sure yours are in good shape and not worn down.

Your round starts the moment you wake up

Whenever I'm playing in a tournament, my round starts as soon as I wake up in the morning. By that I mean that my whole routine and actions are geared to ensuring that I arrive at the course in the correct frame of mind. The last thing I want is to get myself all worked up over something at home so that I turn up at the course stressed out. Try to do the same. Stay calm, leave yourself plenty of time to get to the course so that you can take a leisurely drive playing some relaxing music and still have enough time to go through the pre-round routine I'm about to advocate. As with most things in life, *preparation is everything!*

On competition day—use the range to warm up, not to practice

I never go to the practice range on the day of a tournament to practice. I'm there purely to warm up, stretch my muscles and find myself some rhythm. A tournament is neither the time nor the place to tinker around with your swing.
If you want to work on your game, great. I'm all for that, but your homework should be done in advance during the week at the driving range, not on a Saturday morning 20 minutes before

you're due to tee off in the monthly medal. Use your time at the range before your round to hit a couple of shots with each club in the bag, starting with your wedges, moving up through to the driver, and then back down again to the wedges to restore your rhythm. Resist the temptation to change your swing; it will do you more harm than good.

Hit chips to different targets

I always make a point of hitting a few practice chips before I play, just to brush away the cobwebs, and I suggest you do the same. Don't waste time hitting to just one target—all you'll be doing is grooving your swing to play one particular shot. Instead, pick out four or five different targets and hit a couple of balls to each one in turn so that you get a feel for all kinds of shots.

Get a feel for the greens and hole a short one

My reason for visiting the practice putting green before I tee off is two-fold. First, I'm trying to get a feel for the pace of the greens and, second, I want to give myself some confidence with the short putts. It's very likely that, until you find your range with your irons, your first few putts during the round will be from reasonably long range, so make sure that you've hit a few before you play. I like to take a few balls, choose three different long range pins and, starting with the nearer flag, roll the ball to each one in turn and back again.

The last thing I do before I head to the first tee is hole a short one, just to give me the confidence of seeing the ball hit the back of the hole.

Just before you tee off, hole a short putt on the practice green. It's a confidence builder!

Pre-Round Checklist

- Focus on your round as soon as you wake up

- Remain calm and drive to the course slowly

- Check your equipment: make sure spikes and grips are clean

- Warm up by hitting two shots with each club on the range

- Hit half a dozen chip shots, varying the targets

- Practice a selection of long range putts

- Hole a short one before you head to the first tee

A BRIEF HISTORY OF TURNBERRY

by Donald Steel

STATION HOTEL
TURNBERRY.
Ayrshire.

If anyone asks me were I would most like to spend a golfing holiday by the sea I don't have to think twice—Turnberry. The main reason is that, unlike other great links, you are constantly aware of the sea's presence. Indeed, from a playing point of view, there are times then that awareness is all too real.

The coastal stretch of holes, intermingling turbulent dunes and rocky crags, symbolizes British golf at its best. Although a definition of these matters is impossible, Turnberry's Ailsa course commands a place in the very highest company. Its addition to the Open championship rota in 1977 was the final jewel in the crown, but golfers do not seek pleasure from the game entirely for the challenge a course presents.

They play it far more for the joy of beautiful surroundings and a feeling of escape. In that, Turnberry is beyond compare. Henry Longhurst paid it the ultimate tribute by saying that "in those long periods inseparable from wartime service when there was nothing to do but sit and think, I used often to find myself sitting and thinking of the time when once again we might be playing golf at Turnberry."

Broad green ribbons of fairway contrasting the slender whiteness of the lighthouse. The Isle of Arran's peaks magnifying the glow of sunset. The low form of the Mull of Kintyre and the distant shores of Northern Ireland etched clear and sharp with, all the time, Ailsa Craig, remnant of a volcanic uprising, lapped by a silver sea.

Not that the scene is always quite so entrancing. It is just as often one of haunting mist or driving wind and rain. Turnberry can be six different places. The weather's ever-changing moods can transform it by the hour but that is in keeping with its history. A modern miracle, it tells of constant change.

It "died" and rose again not once but twice after conversion to an airfield in two world wars, its very existence threatened in 1945 when hostilities ceased. At a meeting in the hotel, the directors declared that Turnberry was finished as a golfing center. While they had seen how easily machines could turn a fairway into a runway, they failed to see how it could be turned back again but they reckoned without one man—Frank Hole, Chairman of British Transport Hotels.

He it was who convinced them that their policy backed the soft option and that, with the proper financial compensation from Whitehall, the task of rehabilitation could be faced with confidence. It was strong talk but Hole matched it with strong action. His powers of persuasion made him Turnberry's savior.

Following the breakup of many of the concrete runways, huge scoops and bulldozers restored the movement and feature to the ground so vital in instilling life to any course. Mackenzie Ross, entrusted with the responsibility of design, made plasticine models of the contours, shapes and slopes he wanted, the machine operators then interpreting his wishes with an imaginative and artistic eye.

For men more familiar with demolition and destruction, it was a remarkable exercise of faith but, under the guidance of the chief foreman of the construction team of Suttons of Reading, the results were spectacular; so spectacular, in fact, that is impossible now to see which holes on the Ailsa were once part of the airfield.

The only mercy was that the undulating country fringing the shore survived unscathed but, before moving on to the glories that lay ahead, it is important to unfurl the early pages of a story that has been full of upheaval and costly endeavor. The earliest records are vague but it was undoubtedly the interest that the Marquess of Ailsa had in the game that succeeded in putting Turnberry on the map.

Around the turn of the century, golf had already had a sizable hold at Prestwick where the first Open was held in 1860 and where the Marquess of Ailsa was captain in 1899. The other great name in Ayrshire golf,

A poster from the 1908 Grand Open Golf Tournament advertises "Special Cheap Fares to Golfers."

The 1st Green in 1912.

THE 1st GREEN, TURNBERRY.

Troon, was founded in 1878 although the journey from Turnberry to Troon or Prestwick was quite an undertaking in those days. Nevertheless, the Marquess was hooked enough on the game to build a private course on his Culzean Estate.

It was a development that quickly became popular but the crucial turn in Turnberry's commercial well-being occurred when the Marquess agreed to its takeover by the Glasgow and South Western Railway. It began a link with the railways that lasted over 70 years.

The first necessity was to broaden communications by opening a branch line from Ayr through Turnberry to Girvan, thereby establishing a link from Glasgow as well as a direct sleeper service from London and the Midlands. Whatever modern slogans may tell us, that was the golden age of the train when roads saw few cars and the skies no passenger air traffic. A fine station was

built at Turnberry but it was the construction of the hotel, soon to become world famous, that forged a lasting alliance with the golf. If there is a better situation and combination anywhere, I have yet to find it.

By 1906, the hotel, golf center and railway began to flourish although not all local opinion agreed with the wisdom of it. Even in a country where the game's traditions were well launched, many saw the railway as an intrusion.

In 1903 an Ayr newspaper commented "There are navvies now, gangs of them, defacing the fair surface of Carrick along a route where Carrick looks across to Arran, to Ailsa Craig, to the outer gates of Clyde." The more enlightened view was that it opened up an area of importance, the railway passing through the heart of Burns country and offering stirring sights en route to the Heads of Ayr and Culzean Castle, part of which, many years later, became the Scottish home of General Dwight Eisenhower.

The British Ladies Golf Championship, 1912.

Home Green, Turnberry

In 1918...

Practicing landings on the airstrip at Turnberry during World War I.

Another source of criticism, this time from the Kirk, was the introduction of Sunday golf. This really was a breakthrough. The Old Course at St. Andrews remains shut on Sunday to this day, except on special occasions, but by April, 1909, Turnberry's golfers, Sabbatarians and non-Sabbatarians, had two 18-hole courses—No. One measuring 6,115 yards and No. Two 5,115 yards.

The credit for their layout was always assumed to belong to Willie Fernie whose son, Tom, became Turnberry's first professional. It seems an obvious connection but, no sooner had Turnberry begun to make a name for itself than the clouds of war descended. It was taken over as a training station for pilots of the Royal Flying Corps and other Commonwealth Flying Units. It is to those of them who lost their lives that the war memorial on the hill above the present 12th green was erected.

The hotel was requisitioned during this period as an officers' mess, particularly for Canadians, in contrast to the Second World War when it saw service as a hospital. Altogether, Turnberry was under military control for five years but the dam-

age to the golf courses was nothing like as extensive as it was 30 years later. As soon as the land was relinquished by the War Office, Messrs Carters of Raynes Park built a new No. Two course which became so popular that it ousted the principal course as favorite for visitors and championship events.

Initially, it was the ladies who bestowed their patronage on it for championships. The first was the Ladies' British Open Amateur championship in 1912 and the second in 1921 when Cecil Leitch inflicted on Joyce Wethered her only defeat in the final of a national championship. In his wonderful book, *Golf Between Two Wars*, Bernard Darwin wrote that in the final Miss Wethered played unworthily in the first round. "She had, as I remember it, been a little inclined during the previous day to cut her shots, and this she could not afford to do against Miss Leitch."

However, as vital a match in a championship Darwin described as "memorable," took place on the very first day. "Miss Leitch was confronted by Alexa Stirling, a beautiful player, then American champion, bred at Atlanta, Georgia, where Bobby Jones comes from, and more or less a contemporary of his." Darwin felt that he had never watched a match on a more unpleasant day, going on to say, "and when at last at a late hour I had completed my account of the match on partially sopped pieces of paper, it never reached London. Yet, as a spectacle, it was well worth the wetting."

The Scottish ladies held five championships at Turnberry in the inter-war years, the last of them won by Jessie Anderson (later to become Jessie Valentine) who also won the British title there in 1937, but another significant date in the general story was 1926. In this year, the London Midland and Scottish Hotels Group assumed control from the Glasgow and South West Railways, the responsibility for the courses changing form David Cooper to Arthur Tawle who, in turn, was succeeded by Frank Hole.

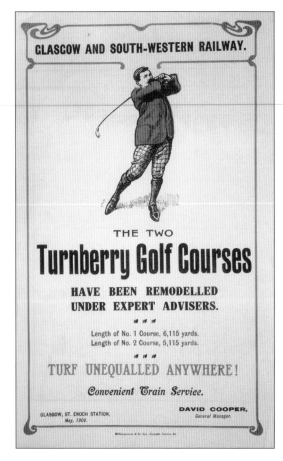

It was at this time that the two courses were christened Ailsa and Arran but Tawle, himself a golfer, was keen that the Ailsa should regain some of its lost popularity and, seeing great possibilities, commissioned Major Cecil Hutchison, one of the masterminds behind Gleneagles, to submit a major redesign that eliminated some of the blind shots and introduced more length.

Bernard Darwin, who referred to it as the "Old" course at Turnberry, felt Hutchison "left it as pretty and charming as he found it, but in a different class as a test of golf." Hutchison therefore could deservedly claim satisfaction and success. The alterations were completed in 1938 but with Hitler already on the march, it wasn't long before all Hutchison's good work was undone.

Turnberry's surrender for a second time to the Air Ministry, or,

more accurately, RAF Coastal Command, was not immediate. It depended, in fact, on a special mission in 1941 whose brief was to look at Turnberry's suitability as a modern airfield. As I wrote in the programme of Turnberry's first Open, "After a good many circuits and approaches in a Spitfire, the opinion of professional flyers not prejudiced by their love of golf was unanimously against the idea. But either the report was blown away along with the corridors of power, or else the Ministry held the belief, not unknown in government, that expert opinion is not to be heeded."

Instead of pitch marks and divots, Turnberry was strewn with skid marks, runways, wind socks and hangars. Whereas in 1914 the airfield was the base for the School of Air Fighting, the last stage of training in what are now regarded as primitive planes, it had to deal in the 1940s with Liberators and Beaufighters which formed part of the anti-

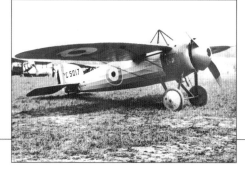

shipping flights. These were principally concerned with U-boat spotting and the dropping

of depth charges. But the charitable opinion that in no way belittles Hutchison's work is that, without the indignities, suffered, a new and more celebrated phoenix might never have arisen from the ashes. Maybe, too, the vision of an Open at Turnberry was the inspiration that guided Frank Hole who sadly died watching the Ryder Cup at Muirfield in 1973, a few months before the announcement of Turnberry's addition to the Open rota.

The prospect facing Hole and Mackenzie Ross in 1948 was gigantic even allowing for their undoubted enthusiasm. During the war, extensive levelling operations had completely flattened large areas. Acres and acres of concrete and tarmacadam, brick and concrete huts, hangars, transformer houses and strong-points disfigured the scene.

Martin Sutton, director of the firm undertaking the work of restoration and author of a notable work, *The Book of the Links*, spent a week surveying the desolation with Ross.

Nevertheless, by the end of it, Ross had decided upon a layout which, it is true to say, confirmed him as an architect to be compared with the best of his distinguished predecessors.

At the end of June, 1949, Suttons were awarded the contract with first priority given to site clearance and to constructing and turfing as many greens as possible in the winter of 1949-50. The summer of 1950 was devoted mainly to the preparation and topsoiling of fairways, construction of bunkers, tees and hillwork, and to the completion of the remaining greens. It was visualized that the greater portion of the work would be finished by the autumn of 1950.

Work actually began towards the end of August, 1949, the biggest job being the removal of the runway foundations which were as much as four feet in depth including a six-inch layer of concrete. Much of the excavated material was used to fill in large holes on other parts of the course and as the foundations for mounds and hills. The rest, many thousands of tons, was carted away to the neighboring village of Maidens and utilized in the construction of a new sea wall.

Excavating concrete on site of approach to the 14th green.

The other major problem was the provision of topsoil lost when the airfield was laid. In some areas, nine inches to one foot had to be found. In all, some 30,000 cubic yards of topsoil was estimated as necessary—normally an impossible request. However, a field adjoining the course had the required amount of light, sandy loam which by horticultural standards might have been regarded as deficient but was ideal for a seaside golf course. With the addition of granulated peat, it proved the answer to a prayer.

Sodding the 7th Green.

In order to make the greens bold and to blend with the surroundings, as much as 4,000 cubic yards of soil were moved for a single green but the end justified the means, particularly with the turfing of every inch of tee, green and fairway. It was a technique never practical enough to have been attempted before or since but by 1951 the Ailsa course had reopened to a justifiable fanfare of trumpets. A dream had come true.

This is not the place for a detailed catalog of the holes, which begin with three that are a pleasant contrast and are the best means of connecting with the sand dune country which shows its hand from the fourth to the eighth. The 9th, 10th and 11th pursue a different stretch of coast but these eight holes comprise the part of the course which visitors remember above everything else.

The 9th is perhaps Turnberry's trademark, the remote tee on the rocks, the drive across the corner of the bay and a glimpse of the site of Bruce's Castle which offers a taste of history in passing. Bruce was an ancient Scottish king remembered by the legend of his spider, one of his castles now depicted by the ruins close to the 9th green and 10th tee.

The narrow path to the 9th tee and the tee shot itself are not to be recommended for those of a nervous disposition. On stormy days it is not even for the strongest and fittest. At one major professional tournament in 1973, which coincided with the autumnal equinox, conditions were so severe that marquees blew down and the world's finest players battled to break 80.

The 1963 Walker Cup competition at Turnberry.

At the first major professional tournament at Turnberry, September 10 through 14, 1957, Henry Cotton plays his second shot on the third fairway in the match against Peter Thomson.

It was more a matter of mental and physical survival than a conventional test of skill. In common with all seaside links, Turnberry needs a little wind to draw its teeth but it would be wrong to convey the impression that the Ailsa peters out once the memorial by the 12th is reached. The 13th and 14th are splendid; the 15th has the same dramatic quality for a short hole as the fourth has while the burn at the 16th, Wee Burn, possesses a menace far in excess of its diminutive title.

Behind the 16th green is one of the spots where the Ailsa and Kintyre courses rub shoulders, the Kintyre replacing the Arran in 2001 as part of Turnberry's twin attractions. The revised Arran, opened in 1954 to a design by Jimmy Alexander, Superintendent of British Transport Hotels' golf courses and the man to whom the credit must be given for the famous, or infamous, back tee on Ailsa's 9th produced the perfect component to his design.

The Arran occupied flatter, more sheltered land than the Ailsa with many holes heavily gorse-lined. Although it was challenging enough to house one of the qualifying rounds for the Amateur championships of 1983 and 1996, it always suffered by comparison with its distinguished neighbour, a situation that finally led to a serious attempt to make it on a par with the Ailsa. The dramatic transformation that resulted was generated by the acquisition of Bain's Hill, land whose elevation added a scenic dimension that not even the Ailsa can match.

This spectacular stretch of rocky coastline added the seaside flavour befitting a links, a character change involving several thrilling shots played against the background of the lighthouse or Ailsa Craig, landmarks symbolic of Turnberry. The elevated perch also gave rise to notable changes of

Michael Bonallack and wife, Angela, in the 1964 British Amateur championship, his first of five victories in the event.

level so lacking on the old Arran, a character transplant that impacted both on the holes themselves and on the celebrated panorama.

In order to make maximum use of pastures new, the old Arran layout was virtually demolished. Only six holes remain recognizably the same and, of these, two had redesigned greens. An additional spin off was that, with the relinquishing of many of the old holes, there was room to establish an additional shorter nine warm-up holes to supplement the extensive practice facilities and golf learning academy. These were all part and parcel of the comprehensive plans submitted along with the proposals to convert the Arran to the Kintyre. Work began in the winter of 1999 and was completed by the following summer.

By the time the Ailsa had reopened in 1951, the railway system had been nationalized although happily Frank Hole remained at the head of Turnberry's affairs as, indeed, he did of Geleneagles and the Manor House at Moretonhampstead. The hotel itself, as photographs show, had expanded after the Second World War, did marvelously well to reestablish its good name but without the renaissance of the golf courses it would have been impossible.

Tom Watson and Jack Nicklaus battled shot-for-shot in the 1977 Open at Turnberry.

Within three years the Scottish Ladies' and Scottish Professional championships had been held there and in 1957 the first of three PGA matchplay championships in six years followed but the Ailsa quickly won favor among the amateurs as well.

The old Amateurs v Professionals match in 1958 heralded the Home Internationals in 1960. and a year later Turnberry housed the Amateur championship for the first time.

It provided Michael Bonallack with the first of his five titles and paved the way for Turnberry's first major international event, the Walker Cup in 1963. Although the Walker Cup match had seen Great Britain and Ireland squander a lead of 7 1/2- 4 1/2 from the first day, it was a great occasion which helped reinforce the body of opinion that the Ailsa was among the finest courses in the land. In this period, the Open championship was growing both in size and importance, a modern Open course having to meet demands of car parking, crowd movement, access by road and rail, and accommodation, as well as being an absolutely first-class test of golf.

No new course had been added to the rota since Royal Birkdale in 1954 but Turnberry's claim grew ever more irresistible and the Royal and Ancient Golf Club's decision to take it there was rewarded in 1977 with what is generally agreed as the most perfect championship ever played. The weather was on its best behavior and the two finest players in the world at the time, Tom Watson and Jack Nicklaus, fought out the most brilliant and dramatic head-to-head confrontation imaginable.

They played shot for shot the last two days, Watson with two rounds of 65 and Nicklaus a 65 and a 66. The difference in the end was that single stroke although both broke the record aggregate for any Open; Watson by eight strokes and Nicklaus by seven. In the second round Mark Hayes' 63 broke the Open's lowest individual round but it was only Watson and Nicklaus who proved inspired throughout. The third place man, Hubert Green, 11 strokes behind Watson, was the only other player to break par for four rounds—adding with a nice touch of humor that he had won the "other tournament."

After so much heartbreak, it was Turnberry's finest hour with the excitement exceeding any script that could have been written. There was an almost fictional touch about the climax as Watson came to the final hole one stroke ahead of Nicklaus. He hit

The 1986 Open.

the ideal iron to the corner of the dog-leg whereas Nicklaus' tee shot drifted towards the gorse. On first inspection, it didn't seem possible that Nicklaus could manufacture any kind of worthwhile shot. When Watson, playing his second first, hit a seven iron which sat down two feet from the hole, that seemed to be that.

However, Nicklaus, somehow, managed to catch an eight iron squarely enough to get his ball to the edge of the green—whereupon he holed it for a three. Watson's putt which minutes before had looked no more than a formality suddenly took on a new dimension but it really was short and, in order to maintain the pattern of perfection, it was right that Watson knocked it firmly home. What happened in that Open took a long time to sink in and the superlatives about it have continued to flow. The filmed version has been shown more times than *Gone with the Wind*. As an exhibition of superb strokeplay, courage and character, it may never be equalled. As an example of all that is good in the game, it was a lesson to other sports.

Although it is hard to know what it could do for an encore, news of the Open's return to Turnberry in 1986 was only a matter of time but there remains one last chapter in the saga of Turnberry and one that carries reassurance and comfort to those anxious to see its future in good hands.

With the sale by the government of the British Transport Hotels chain, Turnberry changed hands twice before becoming part of the Starwood and Westin Hotels Group. In the interim years, the Open championship returned in 1986 and 1994, the same year that a fine new clubhouse was opened by the Duke of York.

Winners of Opens at Turnberry include Nick Price in 1994 and Greg Norman in 1986.

Many alterations and improvements were carried out to the hotel during this period, the most significant being the creation of the Spa but Westin instigated even more extensions with the conversion of the staff houses and flats to further guest accommodation and a new conference centre.

When I first set eyes on Turnberry during the Amateur championship of 1961, I stood transfixed at what I beheld. I have looked out from the hotel over the courses and beyond many times since but the thrill remains as strong; as, indeed, does the thankful acknowledgement that Frank Hole was a man of vision and perseverance.

Turnberry Hotel, Golf Courses and Spa

Ayrshire KA26 9LT, Scotland

Telephone 01655-331000

Turnberry Bay

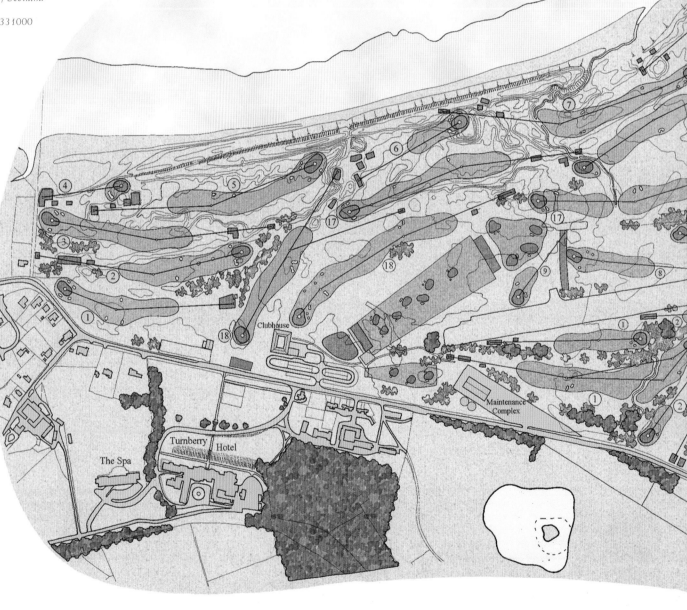

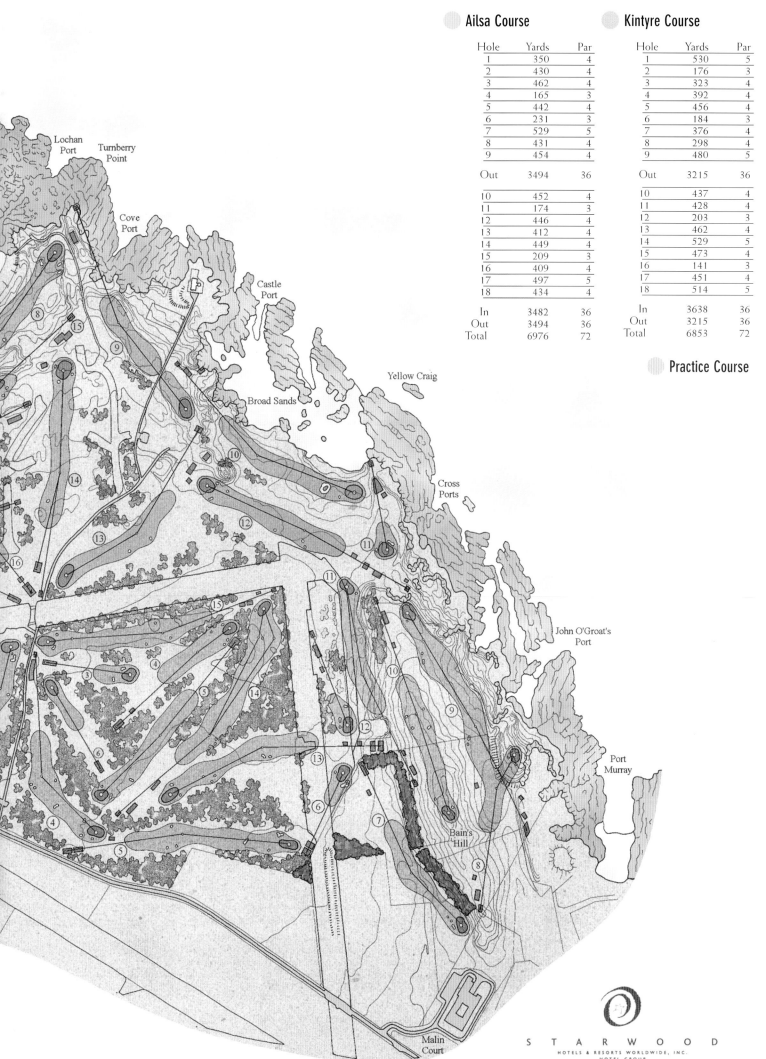

Ailsa Course

Hole	Yards	Par
1	350	4
2	430	4
3	462	4
4	165	3
5	442	4
6	231	3
7	529	5
8	431	4
9	454	4
Out	3494	36
10	452	4
11	174	3
12	446	4
13	412	4
14	449	4
15	209	3
16	409	4
17	497	5
18	434	4
In	3482	36
Out	3494	36
Total	6976	72

Kintyre Course

Hole	Yards	Par
1	530	5
2	176	3
3	323	4
4	392	4
5	456	4
6	184	3
7	376	4
8	298	4
9	480	5
Out	3215	36
10	437	4
11	428	4
12	203	3
13	462	4
14	529	5
15	473	4
16	141	3
17	451	4
18	514	5
In	3638	36
Out	3215	36
Total	6853	72

Practice Course

S T A R W O O D
HOTELS & RESORTS WORLDWIDE, INC.
HOTEL GROUP